# THE
# BOUNDARY-BREAKING
# GOD

# — THE —
# BOUNDARY-BREAKING GOD

## An Unfolding Story
## of Hope and Promise

Danielle Shroyer

**JOSSEY-BASS**
A Wiley Imprint
www.josseybass.com

Published by Jossey-Bass
A Wiley Imprint
989 Market Street, San Francisco, CA 94103-1741—www.josseybass.com

**Library of Congress Cataloging-in-Publication Data**
Shroyer, Danielle, date.
    The boundary-breaking God : an unfolding story of hope and promise / Danielle
Shroyer. — 1st ed.
        p.    cm. — (A living way : emergent visions series)
    Includes bibliographical references.
    ISBN 978-0-470-45100-7 (paperback)
        1. Bible—Meditations.    I. Title.
BS491.5.S56 2009
242'.5—dc22
                                                                            2009018601

Printed in the United States of America
FIRST EDITION
PB Printing      10  9  8  7  6  5  4  3  2  1

**A LIVING WAY**
emergent visions

# Contents

For Mia and Grant

# A Living Way: Emergent Visions Series Foreword

'm dubious of grand, historic-sounding proclamations, but when enough people say that we're in the midst of a spiritual reformation—even an old fashioned revival—it might be time to pay heed. Americans, and people around the world, are not becoming less religious; headlines make that clear. But we are becoming *differently* religious. We're thinking about God in new ways, and we're pioneering new ways to seek after God.

Of course, not all innovations in spirituality are salutary. Some strain the very fabric of the human community. Some tear it.

But others are beautiful and helpful and salubrious. It's these that we desire to publish.

For a decade now, a group of friends has been gathering under the banner "Emergent Village." Officially, we describe ourselves as "a growing, generative friendship of missional Christian leaders." But among ourselves, we know that we're a band of spiritual renegades who have committed to live into the future *together*. We share life in profound ways, we care for one another, and we laugh a lot. I can't imagine a better group of friends.

And out of this cauldron of friendship and disillusion with "religion as usual" have come some ideas and practices that have marked me indelibly. New ways of being Christian, of being spiritual, of following God have bubbled up in this group. We've tried, on occasion, to capture the magic before, like vapor, it slips away. That's not always easy, but sometimes it happens.

Danielle Shroyer has been a faithful member of this group of friends for many years now. When we began, she was an intern at one of the first churches of our movement, and over the years, she has emerged as one of the most potent voices among us. The church she currently leads, Journey, in Dallas, is an exemplary group of Christ followers—a small band of renegades, really, in a city of big steeples and TV preachers. They have fashioned a communion of joy and challenge, and I treasure every time I get to visit them. For her own part, Danielle has brought one of the most potent theologies of the twentieth century, Jürgen Moltmann's theology of hope—to bear on her faith community.

Whether it's evangelical dispensationalism or mainline hand-wringing over denominational collapse, hope seems in short supply in American Protestantism. Danielle's *Boundary-Breaking God* provides a beautiful antidote to waning Christian hope. Herein, Danielle retells the story of God as recorded in the Hebrew and Christian scriptures—a story with which fewer and fewer are familiar—and she does so through the strong biblical themes of hope and promise. It is a story of God pulling us, and all of creation, forward, into the future that is promised by God and inaugurated by Jesus Christ. And as an added bonus, Danielle is a gifted and winsome writer. This book is destined to be praised as a guide to seekers, doubters, wonderers, and believers alike, and it will be read alone and in groups.

Slowly and carefully, we of Emergent Village enter into this realm, and we offer to you, dear reader, our humble attempts at what it means to follow God in this beautiful, worrisome age. We offer "a living way," for we firmly hold that God is alive and active in the world today; our job is to cooperate with what God is already doing. And we offer "emergent visions" because, even as we embrace them as our own in the here and now, we lean into the future, toward which God is beckoning us.

We welcome the conversation that we hope the books in this series will provoke. And we look forward to meeting you down the road so that we can have this conversation together.

Grace and peace to you.

Tony Jones

# Preface

Anne Lamott says she writes novels because some characters in her head just won't leave her alone until she gives them a story. Ideas can be demanding like that. This book, though not a novel, came about in the same kind of way. I have spent a good number of years now reading Scripture, and the stories and themes I have written in this book would not quite leave me alone unless I gave them printed voice. It is such a big, beautiful story, this book we call the Bible. It is tragedy and comedy and human drama and political intrigue and mystery and everyday repetitiveness and a whole web of relationships that endlessly point backward and forward, weaving people and words and events together so that it begins to sound in my head like an old Shaker church choir, singing in the round, its many verses distinct yet harmonious. I have never been fond of religion that tries to make all the verses match.

Pierre Boulez was a French composer in the 1940s who introduced a form of musical composition called "total serialism." It was groundbreaking in that it relied entirely upon mathematical patterns rather than the ear. Even the titles of his works, such as "Structure 1A," insinuated precision over poetry. You have likely not heard of Boulez nor his Structure 1A. That is because his music, though mathematically precise, is not very moving. Without tension and resolution, without a surprising change in octave or a sudden burst of instrumental passion, it ceased to have the transforming dimension that characterizes all truly good music.

Scripture is its own song, and it is a testament to God's good grace that no efforts at "total biblical serialism" have drowned out the tensions and key changes that have always been part of our story.

I am not, in this book, trying to make all the verses match. I do not mean to imply there are not places in Scripture where one could make the opposite claim. The philosopher/debater living in my head had to be edited at every turn to stay on point, rather than traipsing off after every possible rabbit trail of dissent, peeking down into an endless burrow of Ifs and Buts. I *do* mean to say, and I hope rather convincingly, that there is something beautiful, central, even vital about these recurring themes of hope and promise and future in our family book. I do not want to make all the verses match, and I pray I have not (God help me) domesticated them to my own means. I imagine I could write another book structured in this same way, focusing instead on the theme of grace, or justice, or even human folly. As it is, the characters of hope, promise, and future have always been the ones nagging me in my head, so it is their story that I write.

If you happen to be a traditionally church-going person, you will probably notice the trajectory of the book follows the story arc of Scripture—covenant, exodus, and so on. If you happen to be new to this story, consider this a small crash course on some of the high points. These stories loop back toward one another, of course, but they always simultaneously continue forward, press outward, beckon toward the future, pulling each of the stories further along. I believe Scripture does this because in some ineffable way, this is who God is. God weaves people and histories and events and life stories together, referring us backward in remembrance and yet always pushing us toward God's promised future. I hope by sweeping through the grand narrative of God's tale of love with humanity we might see glimpses of God's face in our own stories, too.

If you happen to be a theologian-type, you will probably notice very quickly that I have been influenced greatly by the works of German theologian Jürgen Moltmann. In 1964, his *Theology of Hope* was published.

I did not happen upon it until much later, as a first-year seminary student, but I fell instantly into its pages as if it were a warm, well-worn blanket. All the things I desperately wanted to say about God were sitting on the pages in front of me with language that was roomy and hopeful, just as I believe language about God always should be. Moltmann's works helped me find clarity to describe the story of the God I knew and loved and experienced, to preach the story, to live it. To fully make sense of these themes, however, I needed to comprehend them through the lens of Scripture's narrative arc. In a way, this book is like *Theology of Hope: Bible Edition*. As Moltmann expounded upon these themes in theological structure, I have attempted to do so in narrative biblical form. It has been a delight, as these stories to me are like beloved friends.

Whatever your response to this book, I do pray that the God who has created an ever-expanding universe might be revealed to you in some way in these pages. I especially pray this is true for those of you who may feel that your stories of God have been taken over by something akin to Boulez's total serialism, where doctrinal mechanics and mathematics have pushed out all the poetry that makes this story worth believing. I pray this book will help you find a way to push back, and to reclaim all the space God has given us to roam within the loving embrace of God's sure promise.

# Acknowledgments

As a person who juggles her time between spheres of family, church, and a mild semblance of a social life, writing a book does not simply happen on its own. I am grateful to everyone who filled in the spaces of my life to give me space to write this book. I thank my husband, Dan, first and foremost, who has supported me through this project as well as a long line of projects I have passionately thrown myself into over the years, and has done so with grace and a welcome dash of wit and sarcasm. Thank you for being such a steady comfort and such a good, good man. To my children, Mia and Grant, thank you for being so patient with me on the days I typed more than I played, and for making my life so much more beautiful just by being in it. I am not at all certain how I was given the unbelievable gift of being the mother of such fantastic, fun, bright, and big-hearted children, but I pray for grace as I do my best to honor it. I love you three more than words can say.

To my very large and wonderfully boisterous family, thank you for showering me with such love and encouragement, for sending me notes and e-mails and care packages, for leaving me voicemails to make me laugh, for running carpool duty and taking the kids on outings to give me that extra hour of quiet. I love you all so, so much. To Mom, Dad, and Darren, thank you for allowing me to share a few vignettes of your lives on these pages as well. For my friends, who did a dizzying array of things to make my life easier and functioning brain waves possible—thank you for showing me such love and support.

And of course, deepest thanks to Journey, my beloved community of faith, for being the kind of wonderful people who make pastoral life not only sustainable but truly life giving. It is such an honor to serve as your pastor and to call you friends. Thanks for letting me share glimpses of our life together here, and for all the conversations on Sunday nights, at dinner, and at the Old Monk that have so formed these pages. Special thanks to a wonderful team of leaders—Michael, Jen, Janalee, Dale, Rhealyn, Whitney, John, and Kate—for forcing me to offload some of my pastoral plate as I completed the book and for so joyfully picking up the pieces. And I'm grateful to friend and Journey member Carter Rose, who can snap a photo of absolutely anyone in absolutely any location and make her look like a million dollars. Thanks for sharing your talents so freely.

To Laura Fregin, Jamie Clark-Soles, and a whole slew of Journey members, particularly Bob Pyne and Dale Carter, thank you for providing much needed feedback and encouragement on early and late drafts. Your insights are evident in the final product (and greatly improved the book!), and I am so grateful to have such wise voices in my midst.

Thanks to my first companions at Emergent Village—Rudy Carrasco, Brad Cecil, Tim Conder, Todd Hunter, Tony Jones, Brian McLaren, Jason Mitchell, Sally Morgenthaler, and Doug Pagitt—who a decade ago let a twenty-something theology nerd into their ranks with open arms and showered me with encouragement, wisdom, and much-needed advice. Thanks especially to Tony, who has nagged me to write a book for so long he should receive some kind of medal—both for his persistence and his patience. And thanks to all the new Emergent Village companions I have met along the way, who are far too numerous to mention. I pray the Spirit continues to stir in us a hope for God's world and all the grace and creativity we need to love it as Jesus loves it.

To the fantastic team at Jossey-Bass, thanks for honoring and supporting my words with your efforts.

It truly has been a pleasure to work with you. To Sheryl Fullerton, you have made this process so enjoyable and have most certainly improved my words with your wise guiding hand. Your professional wisdom has been invaluable and your friendship a gift.

# THE
# BOUNDARY-BREAKING
# GOD

# 1

# The Universe Is Moving Outward

I grew up in the wide open spaces of West Texas, where the horizon stretches for miles with nary a tree or building in sight. The word *flat* does not accurately describe it; it is technically a basin. My hometown is situated on what used to be the bottom of a sea floor, the sunken-down middle in a concave bowl of fossil fuels. In this part of the world, the earth is only ten percent of the landscape; the other ninety percent is endless blue sky. We West Texans are known for our unbridled optimism, our refusal to accept limits. The majority of us believe the world is a place where life is always bigger than the dust storm swirling around us, more triumphant than the dry oil well evidences. We believe this because the horizon tells us it is so.

This probably explains why as a child I pictured the world as if it were entirely horizontal. I can still remember learning the story of Christopher Columbus sailing to find the end of the world. Before my teacher could tell us what happened, I began to panic for poor, brave Christopher and his little *Niña, Pinta,* and *Santa Maria* fleet, praying they would not fall off the edge, never to be seen again. My teacher then tried to explain that no such edge exists because we live on a round planet, and if the explorers had not run into various land masses, they could have sailed all the way around and landed right back where they began. I'm sure I looked at her with eyes like saucers. If falling off the edge of the world was far-fetched, I thought, sailing upside down was just plain crazy.

A few years ago, I had another cosmological breakthrough when my husband Dan and I were snuggled up on the couch watching a History Channel documentary about the universe. The documentary chronicled how our views of the world had changed over time from flat earth to round planet, from earth centered to sun centered, from locating the Milky Way to discovering galaxies far beyond the Milky Way. I considered getting up for some popcorn, since this was all pretty standard fare even for a slacker science student like myself. Then they mentioned the Hubble Law, which proved that light stretched the further it traveled, and, the narrator stated matter-of-factly, demonstrated that the universe is expanding.

That's when my mind practically exploded. *The universe is expanding?!* I immediately hopped on a thought train that sent me headlong into the Land of What If. What do you mean the universe is expanding? Into what? Where is it going? Is there some sort of wall we'll hit eventually? What is happening in the empty space we haven't reached yet? Do you mean to tell me that, hypothetically, if my eyes could serve as super-charged telescopes, I could peer upward and watch the cosmos actually growing in size?!

Being a West Texas girl, I had always known the sky was big, but I had no idea the universe was expanding out there farther than I could imagine. It was breathtakingly beautiful to ponder.

God's story is like that. Like the universe, it is always expanding, growing, moving, and being created, even this very moment. I may not have known until that night on the couch that Hubble had a Law more significant than his famous telescope, but I do know this: Through the stories of God's relationship with humanity, we see the same pattern Hubble used as the foundation of his Law—the further we travel into the story of God, the more we see light expanding outward.

The further we travel into the story of God, the more we see light expanding outward.

# A PEOPLE OF PROMISE

As a child, I collected Bible stories like other children collect rocks or baseball cards. Every story fascinated me, and I began amassing them in such a way that my God-story-closet practically bulged both from volume as well as disorganization. In a family like mine, this wasn't difficult to do.

My father hails from the tumbleweeds of West Texas and grew up attending a Southern Baptist church, but Dad is not a churchy kind of guy. For one thing, he's a rock-and-roll musician, so he would much rather play Johnny B. Goode than sing "Amazing Grace" with painfully slow organ accompaniment. Then there was the time Mom convinced him to go to Sunday School, and when the teachers separated the husbands and the wives, Dad yelled, "What for? They think we're going to get frisky in the middle of Sunday School or something? Hell, if I wanted to do that, I'd at least go out to the parking lot!" My brother and I found this story hilarious, but Mom was slightly less amused. We may not have gone to church every Sunday, but we talked about God's stories before bedtime and around the dinner table, my dad freely inserting comical side commentary at will.

My mother is Lebanese. All of the ancestors on my mother's side are Druze, a far-removed descendant of Shi'a Islam, which, like Judaism, is both ethnic and religious. My grandparents lived all over the world, in places with such differing religious cultures as Africa, Mexico, and, of course, the Middle East. They were as Druze as you can get culturally, but they did not practice Druze religion with the same enthusiasm.

When Mom began to inquire more about the Druze faith, she quickly became disenchanted with the stark hierarchy that prevented her as a woman from being educated about Druze beliefs. In her twenties, she made a radical and life-changing decision to become a follower of Jesus, and all of her siblings, as well as my grandmother, followed suit.

In addition to our experiences at church on Sundays, my brother and I attended an Episcopal private school where we encountered all the "smells and bells" of formal church, with Latin hymns and communion with wine in fancy glass jars and thin wafers embossed with tiny crosses. Between the stories of God I heard at church, at school, and in my spiritually eclectic family, I had quite a collection.

It was not until studying religion in college that I learned how to sort Scripture stories—prophets over here, Jesus stories over there, letters from the early church in this pile, poems and songs in that one—and line them up in order. Arranging them that way helped me see and hear the cadence and rhythm not just of each little story but of the big, ongoing story, so that it began to resemble a symphony, its themes both recurring and amplifying as the song goes on. When you experience the story as a whole, you can see the trajectory of God's horizon expanding outward and practically hear it crescendo.

At every turn, a promise propels God's song toward its next peak. Promises might appear small to us, but they are the catalysts of God's story. Think of it this way: If the universe is accelerating outward, pushing the rewind button on cosmic history suggests it began as a small, outrageously dense particle of energy. Scientists call this particle a *singularity*. In God's story, it is called a *promise*.

I realize we are not used to taking promises quite so seriously. We find them easy to overlook, probably because we're often all too ready to let ourselves off the hook when it comes to keeping them. But God approaches promises with much greater gravitas. In God's story, promises are the activation seeds of God's future, the energy particle that launches the story further out.

> n God's story, promises are the activation seeds of God's future, the energy particle that launches the story further out.

To follow the arc of God's expanding promise, we begin with a nomadic couple named Abraham and Sarah who lived with their families in the town of Haran. God came to them there and

6

promised to make them a great nation, through whom
all the families on earth would be blessed. There was
just one problem. Abraham and Sarah were old, and they
could not bear children. How could they birth many
nations when they couldn't even bear a single child? For
reasons unknown, Abraham and Sarah chose to trust in
God's promise, and that was the beginning of the great
covenant. It may have begun with one couple, but the
relationship the great covenant forged would eventually
activate a relationship between God and all of creation.
Abraham and Sarah packed up their belongings and
traveled to a new land, Canaan, the place God promised
would hold their future.

The journey was not easy. After many years of
traveling and moving and facing disappointment month
after month as they failed to conceive, they became
rightly discouraged. One night Abraham lamented to
God, and God beckoned him outside. "Do you see all
those stars?" God asked. "*That* is how many children I
promise you will have." Abraham looked up at the vast
desert sky, and in that immense horizon he somehow
found space to believe again in this grand promise.

Years passed again until Abraham had reached the
age of ninety-nine. He was preparing to take an after-
noon nap under the cool shade of the oak trees at the
entrance of his tent when he saw three men standing
before him. Abraham greeted them and, with customary

hospitality, he invited them to stay for dinner. The three guests obliged, and Abraham hurried to ask Sarah to help him prepare food for their surprise company. When the food was ready, Abraham served the men, who were reclining under the oak trees. One of them remarked, "Where is your wife Sarah?" Abraham pointed through the crack in the tent curtain and said, "In the tent." The visitor remarked, "The next time I come around this way, your wife Sarah will have a baby."

Now Sarah could hear the men talking as she worked in the tent, and when she heard what the stranger said, she could not help but laugh. Imagine such a thing! A baby, at her age, after all this time? She could hardly believe in a promise that had long since grown cobwebs at that place of hope in her heart. The stranger heard her laugh and turned to Abraham. (Here the previously unnamed traveler is identified as God, so quietly that you almost miss it altogether.) God said, "Why did Sarah laugh? Is anything too wonderful for the Lord? Trust me—she will have a son." Sarah, now feeling awkward that her moment of laughter alone in the kitchen was overheard, and being afraid of what punishment might meet her ridicule, denied it, saying, "I didn't laugh." But God, like a mother amused when her child claims innocence with dirt plainly on his hands, said, "Oh, yes you did." (And with a little sass, too, I imagine.) Luckily, Sarah was not alone in her doubt; when

Abraham received a vision about this very promise not long before the three travelers showed up, he had laughed, too. It was only fitting, then, when this long-promised child was finally born, that they name him Isaac, which means, "he laughs."

In time, Isaac met and married Rebekah, and they had twin sons, Jacob and Esau. Jacob, the favored one, then had twelve of his own: Asher, Benjamin, Dan, Gad, Issachar, Joseph, Judah, Levi, Naphtali, Reuben, Simeon, and Zebulun. From these twelve children, one family expanded into the twelve tribes of Israel. Each child received a portion of territory, and each tribe expanded and multiplied until their numbers were very great. The covenant that began with Abraham and Sarah now expanded to include twelve very well-populated tribes. The promise was picking up speed.

## FINDING GOD'S HORIZON

If we imagine the story of God as a symphony with recurring themes that amplify as the song continues, its chorus would most certainly be "Go!" The promises of God send us places because God is on the move. When God first came to Abraham and Sarah, God called them to leave what they knew and move toward a promised new future. God didn't give a lot of details about what

Canaan, their new home, would be like, or even what the journey would be like. God just said, "Go," and off they went. We will hear this chorus frequently as we travel through God's story, because God told a lot of people to go—farmers and mothers, prophets and princesses, fishermen minding their own business and women retrieving water from wells and a whole slew of shepherds just trying to keep their flocks together. Jesus told people to go so often you can hardly read a few lines in the Gospels before running across the directive, which is why it isn't remotely surprising that one of Jesus' last words to the disciples is—that's right—"Go." God moves ahead of us and pushes us from behind at every juncture of the story, because we are part of this great movement out toward God's promised future.

We are part of this great movement out toward God's promised future.

The circumstances of why and where God calls and sends people are incredibly diverse, but the fact that the story of God spends such an enormous amount of time talking about people moving and leaving what is comfortable or familiar for something new is probably worth our attention and consideration. I have a hunch there is something about human nature itself that needs a horizon. If you think about times in your life where there has been despair, it's most likely because you lost

sight of the future. You couldn't imagine what life would
be like without someone, or you didn't know what you
were going to do with your life, or you weren't sure
where you belonged anymore. Despair happens when
our horizon begins to look and feel more like a cave.
Although it often feels completely counterintuitive,
when we most want to shut ourselves off and stay in
our own caves, the fog of sadness begins to lift when we
are ready to go out—moving outside of ourselves, serving others, thinking about something other than what
feels like a horizon-less existence. We need to go somewhere and find the sky again.

This is one of a million mysterious ways I believe
God has created us in God's own image. We are created
to be as dynamic as the God who made us. We are created to move toward the future.

Just to be clear, to say God's future moves outward
is not to say that humanity is slowly moving to perfec-
tion. The depressing truth is that despite all our achieve-
ments, the twentieth century was possibly the bloodiest
in human history, so any notion that we are getting
better is not entirely tuned into reality. Maybe God has
to tell us to go so often because we repeatedly head in
the wrong direction. If we truly want to participate in
the movement of God in the world, we have to start
by acknowledging the world as it is, broken as well as
beautiful. We have to accept that we may be going, but

we may not be going the right way. Finding God's horizon and walking toward it is a spiritual practice that requires willing and persevering feet. Thankfully, God seems fully aware that our feet will get tired, that we will become impatient, that there will be long patches when we fear God has forgotten about us and left for the beach. When Abraham was downtrodden, God did not say, "Cheer up! Everything is going great! Who's having fun yet?" God came to Abraham right in the middle of his sadness, lifted his gaze and said, "Do you remember what I promised?" We follow God not because things are always going so smashingly well, but because we trust the promise that looms on God's horizon.

Scripture tells the story of a God who promises us a future, most especially when the world looks dark. When we look up into the sky, we know we are looking toward the future, and we find hope in the promise of God. We trust God is taking us—all of us—toward something, and we trust it is worth the journey. We are a people who speak openly of what was and frankly about what is, but we live as those who believe what will be.

# 2

# The God of Green Lights

I was probably six. As I stood with my toes hugging the lip of the swimming pool in the back yard of my best friend's house, I wanted more than anything in the entire world to dive in. I could picture it in my head—my arms making a graceful triangle above my head as my hands entered the water without so much as a splash. But no matter how well it went in my mind, my toes still gripped the edge. I didn't move. It didn't help that the three sons of my best friend's family—Wagner, Weston, and Wilson, as well as my brother Darren—were splashing wildly around in the water and occasionally taunting me with scaredy-cat jokes. I could hold my own just fine when we had wrestling matches on an old mattress in the playroom upstairs. I fought those matches with every ounce of my sad little underweight self. I could pinch like a champ, and they would scream like babies when I tried to rip out their burgeoning leg hair. But the pool was a different matter.

"Hey Danielleopi," they yelled. "Want us to give you a little push?" I tried to glare at them with Rocky Balboa–like fierceness. "I can do it myself," I retorted. But forcing yourself to jump is much harder than it seems. Sometimes, you do need a little push, which is the only reason that I remained on speaking terms with Weston after he snuck over and shoved me in.

To move toward God's horizon, we have sometimes needed a push, too. God calls us to go, and sometimes, like Abraham and Sarah, we go without hesitation. Other times, even when a cool pool of freedom awaits, we can't seem to detach our toes from the edge. What happens when we find ourselves stuck, either because of oppressive outside forces or the fears lodged in our own heads? The story of the Israelites' exodus from Egypt tells us something about both.

To move toward God's horizon, we have sometimes needed a push.

# FAITHFUL DISOBEDIENCE

God made the grandest of all promises to Abraham and Sarah when God said that through them, all nations would be blessed. God called them to go, and they dislodged their feet from home and set out toward the green light of God's future. God expanded that promise by giving them a child, Isaac, and through Isaac, Abraham and Sarah's family grew into twelve tribes.

During a time of severe drought, much of Israel moved to Egypt, because Egypt had storehouses of food stockpiled in preparation for the crisis (thanks to Joseph, the great-grandson of Isaac . . . but that's another story). While in Egypt, the tribes continued to increase, and the new pharaoh decided to confront this threat before it got out of hand. Pharaoh forced the Israelites into slavery. He placed taskmasters over them to ensure their obedience, and he kept them so busy they had little time to think of anything else. But the Israelites continued to increase, which made Pharaoh all the more nervous. Finally, in order to squelch the possibility of revolt, Pharaoh decided to do more. He summoned all the midwives who assisted Hebrew (Israelite) women, and he told them to kill every baby boy that was born. In essence, he was trying to kill the Israelites' future. Babies are like tiny packages of hope, cries of promise for what can be. If you're Pharaoh and you want to limit the Israelites' ability to imagine a future any different from the one you choose to give them, it's best not to have babies around. If you can somehow figure out a way to do this and shift the blame elsewhere, all the better. The way I see it, Pharaoh wanted the midwives to help birth the babies, then kill them and tell the mothers there were complications during the birth. Death during childbirth was so common you can imagine why Pharaoh might have considered it such a foolproof plan.

Unfortunately for Pharaoh, two Egyptian midwives named Shiphrah and Puah refused to obey. Word eventually got back to Pharaoh that Hebrew baby boys were making appearances around town, so he summoned Shiphrah and Puah to his court and asked them why they allowed the boys to live. Those two plucky women, in a bold response that sounds almost comedic, looked at Pharaoh and said, "These Hebrew women aren't like Egyptian women. They are strong and hearty, and they birth those babies before we have a chance to get there." As far as we can tell, Pharaoh must have bought this line, because the midwives were released without punishment. It was definitely not the end of the story, however.

Because of the midwives' disobedience, Pharaoh was forced to show his hand. He could not secretly kill the Hebrew babies, so he issued a decree to all of Egypt that all Hebrew baby boys should be drowned in the Nile. The book of Exodus doesn't tell us what the overall response was to this horrifying decree. Perhaps Shiphrah's and Puah's righteous disobedience spurred more people to refuse Pharaoh's paranoid orders. We know for certain what one mother did.

A woman named Jochebed hid her sweet baby for three months, until she couldn't hide him any longer. Then she got a basket and lined it with tar and blankets and gently put him inside. She went down to the river and placed him among the reeds, and her daughter Miriam followed the basket as it floated downstream. Pharaoh's daughter happened to be bathing at the river, and she saw the basket and heard the baby boy crying inside. Her heart melted when she saw that baby, knowing he was the son of a mother desperate to keep her child alive. She drew the baby out of the water and named him Moses (which means "to draw out"), and she raised him in the palace of the very king who had decreed his death.

We don't know much about Moses' childhood, because the next thing we read in the book of Exodus, Moses is fully grown. One day, while he was outside the palace walls, Moses saw an Egyptian beating an Israelite and was outraged. He looked around to make sure he was alone, and then he killed the Egyptian and buried him in the sand. (Sometimes that part gets left out in Sunday School.) The next day Moses went out again, and he saw two Israelites who were fighting, so he approached them and said, "Why would you strike one of your own like that?" One of them replied, "Who made you judge? Are you going to kill me like you did that Egyptian?"

Unfortunately for Moses, the Hebrew slave wasn't the only one who knew about what he had done. It turns out Pharaoh knew as well, and he was looking to kill Moses as punishment. Moses fled from Egypt to Midian, where he stayed until Pharaoh died.

Meanwhile, the Israelites continued to endure the hardships of slavery. The book of Exodus says their cries rose up to God and God heard their groaning and remembered the covenant, the great promise God had made with all the Israelites. Then God did a remarkable thing. God came to visit Moses, the exiled murderer, while he was tending sheep. God spoke to Moses through a bush that was burning and yet not consumed by fire. God called Moses by name and said, "Moses, I have heard my people crying. I have come to deliver them and to bring them out of that land of slavery into a land that will be wide open and free. Go to Pharaoh so that we can rescue my people out of Egypt."

Moses wasn't entirely convinced this plan was a good one. He suffered from a speech impediment and was terrified it would surface in the palace for everyone to hear. And his criminal record did not exactly pave

the way for a heartfelt homecoming. But God sent him
anyway. So Moses, once a palace resident, came again to
stand in front of the new pharaoh and demand freedom
for God's people. Moses stood before Pharaoh ten times
and told him, "The God of Abraham says, 'Let my people
go.'" And ten times, Pharaoh said no. Only in the wake
of ten horrible plagues did Pharaoh finally heed God's
command to let the Israelites go.

Moses had instructed the Israelites to be ready to
leave at a moment's notice, and they were ready. They
rushed from their homes and headed out toward the
Red Sea, fearful that Pharaoh would change his mind
and come after them. And wouldn't you know it,
Pharaoh did exactly that. He probably got to thinking
about all that free labor he was losing, all that profit and
power he would relinquish. He groaned, "What have
we done?" and he sent chariots and horses to bring the
Israelites back.

The Israelites were all gathered at the edge of the
Red Sea, and as they looked over their shoulders, they
saw the Egyptians gaining ground, coming right toward
them, and they completely panicked. They began yell-
ing at Moses, "What have you done to us? Were there
not enough graves in Egypt, so you thought it would be
better for us to die out here in the wilderness, Moses?
We told you to leave us in Egypt and let us remain
slaves!" (Personally, I would have said something like,

"Hey Moses, next time you decide to be our big hero, how about you find us a route that does not entail getting us trapped between a river and an angry mob of our enemies?") Moses replied, "Don't be afraid. God's going to deliver us, just be calm . . . and wait!" I imagine the Israelites looked at him with glares that could be translated, "You have *got* to be kidding. You want us to stand here and do *nothing?*" God agreed with them on this point. God said to Moses, "What are you waiting for? *Go!* Lift up your staff and stretch out your hands to divide the sea and *go!*"

Moses did what God said, and God parted the waters right down the middle. The people of Israel ran across dry ground to the other side and found themselves facing the horizon of their freedom. God had given them a green light, and no army, no king, no sea, would stop them.

## LEARNING TO BE FREE

The exodus story tells us that God stands with the downtrodden and demands they be let go. God's story moves us outward, but like the Israelites, we still encounter roadblocks along the way. We certainly don't have to search very far to confront the injustices in our own world—Pharaohs who hang their power threateningly over our heads, evil systems like slavery that seem insurmountable. The red lights of human tyranny are real, but God's future always calls us—pushes us, even—to move toward justice.

The exodus is also a story about our fears. Plunging into God's future can be riskier than staying where we are. That's why much of God's story in the Bible is a story of learning how to be free. God makes a way for us, but we have to do the walking. We have to leave our homes, flee across the floor of the Red Sea, and find our way in the desert as we travel toward the Promised Land.

Much of God's story in the Bible is a story of learning how to be free.

And when we arrive, sometimes the freedom of the wilderness feels foreign to us. We've gotten so used to the bars of slavery around our souls we feel almost vulnerable without them. We want to be free, desperately, but we don't always know how.

To make matters worse, we are often oblivious to what enslaves us. For the Israelites, Pharaoh was a pretty obvious target. But Pharaoh himself was a slave, too—a slave to his stubbornness, to his desire for power, to his fear of losing control, and he couldn't see it even after being confronted with it ten times in a row. When God pushed Pharaoh until he let the Israelites go, God was shoving Pharaoh's unwilling feet toward freedom, too.

Jesus tells us that to be free we have to practice two things: loving God and loving our neighbors as ourselves. This sums up every other practice in God's story. It also is the shorthand version of the Ten Commandments.

When we talk about the Ten Commandments at Journey, the community I pastor in Dallas, we describe them as ways that show us how to be free. I know some of you may think, "Aren't they a list of things not to do? Don't they construct a kind of religious prison?" Some people may use them that way, but that certainly wasn't what was intended. In the story of the exodus, the Israelites quickly realized they did not know how to live as free people. This generation had never tasted freedom, and freedom can be very disorienting at first. Often our initial reaction is to run headlong toward the familiar. Look at what happened when the Israelites got to the edge of the Red Sea. They demanded Moses return them to Egypt so they could live as slaves again. Even after they crossed the Red Sea successfully, it hardly took any time at all before they began to miss the "perks" of living in Egypt. "Oh, the meals we had!" they exclaimed. Three square prison meals a day! And they were stuck out in the wilderness having to worry about their own food. They grumbled to Moses and asked him why he ever took them to this Godforsaken wilderness at all.

When people protectively hug the bars of slavery, nothing short of a life revolution is necessary. Looking back to romanticize the past was never going to do the Israelites any favors. They needed to find the horizon again and start walking. The Ten Commandments were given as signposts on the road toward freedom, a call to keep on walking toward the Promised Land, and to imagine a different kind of life defined not by slavery but by a life-giving relationship with God and each other.

Walking the way of God's freedom is not easy. Pharaohs and other outside forces of injustice attempt to blind us with their flashing red lights, and we have internal red lights to contend with as well. Battling both of these requires a lot of work, and sometimes we don't feel entirely up to it. Every year at Lent, the season of preparation for Easter, Journey members offer up a collective groan as we gear up for forty days of intensive introspection. We groan not because we dislike Lent (well, maybe a few do!) but because Lent requires us to concentrate our attention on all that enslaves us and all we have done to enslave others. It can be a pretty long list when we're brave enough to be honest with ourselves. Each year on Ash Wednesday night, we receive ashes on our foreheads in the form of a cross. "Repent and live the good news," I pray over each of the community members as they come forward, and we sit quietly, marked by our ashes, praying that the humanity we bear might be the humanity of Jesus. We take up our humanity, broken as it is, with the shadow of a Pharaoh lurking in each of us, with our knuckles pale from holding on to things we should have let go of a long time ago. We take up our humanity, and we remember that we are God's people, with God's image living in us, and we have been set free, sent forth. For forty days we practice being free from all that traps us at the water's edge, and we remember that God is on our side.

God is on the side of human wholeness and not human corruption. Slavery and domination, abuses of power—these are gruesome caricatures of humanity. These are forces with no horizon, no future, only endlessly repeating patterns of distress. God liberates us so that we can once again be fully human in the most God-created sense of the word—humans who reflect the image of the God who has created us, humans who live as life bearers and life givers, siding with hope, grace, peace, and love. In the power of God's promise as the true liberator, the One who rescues us from a life of slavery and offers us a life of freedom, we are given a hopeful horizon.

## CHOOSING LIFE

One of my friends often uses the phrase, "It is what it is." He says this mostly when something doesn't make any sense or feels overwhelming, and it is almost always accompanied with a shrug. Personally, I accidentally killed a bird a few years ago when it flew headlong into the front of my car, and I cannot even say "It is what it is" about that, so I'm perhaps a little biased in believing this is not always a helpful response. However, it seems rather obvious that the exodus story would have been very different if God heard all those cries of the Israelites and replied, "It is what it is." God doesn't shrug at suffering. God is not resigned to the brokenness of the world but is intent on bringing healing and wholeness back to all of creation. As a person who follows God, I cannot look upon the violence of this world and say, "It is what it is." I must say, "This should not be." I am not called to accept violence with a helpless shrug but to feel the deep despair of it, to be pulled toward action because of it, to imagine a future without it. The call of God's future evokes our desire to pursue justice, to live like what we do and how we choose to live truly matters. We do not follow a God who says, "It is what it is," but the God who says, "I am who I am." And who God is in the exodus story is a God who hears the cries of those who suffer and responds. If we are to follow God, we are called to do the same.

We do not follow a God who says, "It is what it is," but the God who says, "I am who I am."

If we care about God's horizon of freedom, we will walk toward it with all the faith we can muster and help others walk toward it, too. When the gruesome realities of injustice hold us captive at the edge of the shore, we have to use our imaginations and dive into the hope of a different future, of God's future. We get the courage to go when we refuse to accept the world as it is and dare to imagine what it can be, what it should be. Slavery, in its many deceptive forms, robs us slowly of our imaginations. If we want to move toward God's horizon, we must find ways to reject the cages of slavery as lasting or permanent and shake off our indifference. When Shiphrah and Puah refused to follow Pharaoh's orders, they didn't just save babies. They rejected Pharaoh's attempts to constrict their imaginations. When Pharaoh's daughter opened her heart to love a Hebrew baby as her own, she denied her father's oppressive power and made space for a new story instead.

Ann Ulanov once said that violence is often the result of a lack of imagination. I think we could say the same thing about injustice. Injustice and violence happen when we limit our view of what is possible and resign ourselves to accept that the world "is what it is." They happen when our horizons get obscured, or when they cease to be God's horizons, which is to say the same thing. Utilizing our own powerful sense of hope, grounded in the very real promises of God, is to imagine and therefore bring into being a life of freedom.

It's in the book of Deuteronomy that we read the
story of the Israelites who had been traveling in the wilderness for forty years, waiting to go into the land God
had promised them. They were camped out on the plains
of Moab near the Jordan River, and they would soon
cross over water once again, this time to enter the land
of Canaan. Remember, Canaan is where God promised
Abraham and Sarah their future would be, and all these
years later, the time had finally arrived. It was a pivotal
moment, one that deserved a speech. Moses gathered the
Israelites together. He reminded them of the promises
God made to Abraham and Sarah. He reminded them
of the covenant that God would be their God and they
would be God's people. He reminded them of all the
good things that had happened over the past forty years,
and all of the bad. He reminded them of all the ways
God had provided a way for them, even when they had
lost all hope. He reminded them of their responsibility
to live as the free people of God and to be a blessing to
the whole world. It was a really long speech, and Moses
must have realized how overwhelming all those responsibilities sounded when he added, "And don't you dare
tell me this is too hard to do. It isn't in heaven where
you can't reach it, or across the sea where you can't go.
No—the word is very near to you; it's in your mouth
and in your heart. So here it is, I'm setting two choices
before you today—life and death. *Choose life.*"

We are called not only to remember the exodus, but more important, to practice it. We are called to fill our world with exodus moments in which God's horizon replaces injustice and oppression. We are called to choose life. In every decision we make, we have to ask ourselves, What will bring about life? And not any kind of life, but the power of life that comes from following the Liberating God. Our journey toward freedom cannot be the substitution of one kind of slavery for another. We cannot leave Pharaoh and then become pharaohs of our own, doing as we please without concern for anyone else. Selfishness is its own wilderness, where the beauty of freedom still eludes us. To be truly free, as told in God's unfolding story, is to belong to our God and belong to each other. Jesus reminded us of the signposts to freedom we had been given in the Ten Commandments, where we are called to live in a network of relationships between our God and our neighbor. Jesus, too, reminded us to choose life. Loving God and loving one another certainly costs us something, and yet, it is the only true currency that will endure. We are called to practice exodus, to practice letting God's people go, and to practice the going.

> We are called to fill our world with exodus moments.

Nobody is allowed to get in the way of God's call for us to go. And when we see injustice, we are called to act like Moses and confront the pharaohs of our own day. We are called to be people who practice exodus day after day after day. We have seen freedom fighters decry the pharaoh of American slavery. We have seen Martin Luther King Jr. galvanize the fight against the injustice of racism and suffragettes denounce the injustice of sexism. We can tell stories of economists working in the Two-Thirds World to bring about economic exodus in small villages through sustainable efforts. We can hear about American teenagers emboldened by the plight of child soldiers in Uganda and raising their voices to a shout. In each of these ways, and in countless more, we declare and demand the future of God to be made more present among us. When we practice exodus, we declare our allegiance not to the powers that be but to the God of Green Lights.

# 3

# We Come Bearing Gifts

For as long as I can remember, my parents' house has been filled with camels. I don't mean there is one curio cabinet of camel figurines tucked in the dining room corner. I mean no matter where you stand in my parents' house, if you look in any direction, chances are you will see at least one camel. When I've brought people home with me in the past, they have often asked, "What's with all the camels?" Usually I tell them, "Well, we're Lebanese," as if *all* Lebanese people stuff their houses with dromedaries as a matter of course. Actually, my mom just really likes camels. Your mom might have a few little bunny statues sitting around, or perhaps some Precious Moments figurines somewhere. My mom has a thing for camels.

It's my dad I blame for the overwhelming number of camels, though. Whenever my brother and I were out shopping with him, we were required to be on the lookout for dromedary discoveries. If we found one, Dad would pay for it when Mom wasn't looking and would smuggle it into the car with a mischievous grin on his face. If during one of our secret camel-searching missions we happened to run across a set of the three wise men on their camels, my dad would auspiciously shout, "Jee-*ack-pot!*" in his West Texas twang. Three camels in one! This was the mother lode.

As strange as it may sound, I like having the camels around. I feel a kinship with them, as if they somehow hold the connection between the world of my mother's ancestors and my own very different world. My favorite camels were the Christmas camels saddled with gifts and colorfully dressed riders. You may have heard the story about three wise men who follow a star to find the baby Jesus. It doesn't get much attention outside of a minor shout-out during a Christmas Eve service and the occasional rendition of the Christmas hymn "We Three Kings," but you can be sure they are on the front of our family Christmas cards every year.

Given my childhood fondness for camels, you can probably imagine my absolute sheer and total delight when I discovered in seminary there was an entire holiday devoted to the wise men and their dromedary friends. People casually mentioned this "Epiphany" holiday as if it were a matter of course, so I tried to play it cool, as if I had not just stumbled upon the best news ever. I secretly went home, researched it and wondered how it was possible to get this far in my field without even knowing about Epiphany. Now, I make up for lost time every year on Epiphany, when Journey members endure my exuberance as I talk about why this story is so beautiful and why it matters so much.

Most people who know this story zoom right past it, as if it's a window display they have seen before. They have not stopped to peer inside, to notice the details, and to consider what it indicates about where the story of God might be heading. For most, these men and their camels are simply pieces people use to populate their nativity scenes, making the Jesus-in-the-manger barn scene look more crowded and important. Very few realize what a grandiose political statement it is to place ceramic painted figurines of pagan men holding gifts in front of this Jewish king. It is not simply holiday cheer; it is a prophetic statement about the kind of world God is creating.

What a grandiose political statement it is to place ceramic painted figurines of pagan men holding gifts in front of this Jewish king.

I should just tell you the story, and you will see what I mean.

Tradition says there were three wise men, but we don't know how many there were. Most likely, there were far more than just three. Also, people usually call them wise men, or magi, or kings, but those are all nice ways of evading the fact that they were pagan astrologers. They looked at stars and interpreted current and future events. If they had not been astrologers, they never would have stumbled upon a strange-looking star in the eastern sky that landed them, oddly enough, in the pages of the Bible.

One day, these astrologers were peering into the night sky, as they were wont to do, and they found a star they did not recognize. I imagine they knew most of the stars they saw every night, so when a new, bright star popped up, it caught their attention. Somehow, they must have stumbled on a Jewish prophecy that talked about a star in the eastern sky foretelling the birth of the Messiah King. This is a little bit far-fetched when you consider these astrologers did not live near Jerusalem, and life back then wasn't exactly well connected. If something wasn't going on in your town or general surrounding area, chances are you wouldn't know about it. And though most of us are at least marginally aware of the people and places mentioned in the Bible,

Judaism wasn't a widely known world religion at the time. So the idea that these astrologers found any Jewish prophecy at all is pretty remarkable.

Even more remarkable, however, is that they were so intrigued by the star and the prophecy that they loaded up their camels for the long journey to Jerusalem and brought gifts befitting a king. (They chose Jerusalem, of course, because where else would the Jewish King be?) This would be like one of us traveling fifteen hours on an airplane to a small, relatively unknown country for the inauguration of a king with whom we have no connection and whose rule we certainly don't live under—and bringing him bags of goodies from Neiman Marcus, jewelry from Tiffany and Co., and perhaps some scented candles from Bergdorf Goodman.

I don't know what the wise men were expecting when they arrived in Jerusalem, but I can imagine that they assumed they would be joining an enthusiastic celebration heralding the birth of this new king. But when they reached the streets of Jerusalem, there was no celebration in sight. It seemed as if nothing in Jerusalem had changed at all. Imagine how disoriented they must have been to discover they were the only partygoers in town! The astrologers made their way through the city streets, asking complete strangers, "Where is the child who has been born King of the Jews? We saw his star as it was rising, and we've traveled all this way to worship him." It goes without saying that foreign astrologers speaking of the Jewish Messiah King on the streets of Jerusalem had to have seemed unbelievably strange as well as presumptuous. If you happened to be the resident king, it also was likely alarming.

It did not take long for news of these strange outsiders to reach the courts of King Herod, and he was not pleased. This is the king who celebrated his appointment by the Romans by slaughtering every last member of the Sanhedrin, the Jewish court, because he felt they had too much influence. The talk of any new king was likely enough to rattle Herod, but the fact that it came from astrologers who had traveled halfway across the world must have been terrifying. Herod summoned the Jewish chief priests to his court to find out more about the situation, but the chief priests were probably just as confused. They were also in a very compromising spot, considering Herod had murdered their friends in similar positions. They knew Herod would not stand for talk of a Messiah who would deliver the Jews from foreign domination and whose throne would have no end, as prophecies of the Messiah often said. The chief priests needed to come up with an inoffensive answer—quickly.

I've always wondered why they didn't tell Herod about Isaiah 60:6, which reads, "A multitude of camels shall cover you; they shall bring gold and frankincense and shall proclaim the praise of the Lord." They knew of it, most certainly, and it seems pretty obviously applicable to the situation at hand. Maybe they were worried Herod wouldn't let them end with that verse, and they would have to keep reading to the part about nations and kings streaming to Jerusalem to bring offerings and service to God. You can imagine how that would go over.

Instead, the chief priests referred Herod to Micah 5:2. "And you, Bethlehem, are certainly not the least in the land of Judah; for from you will come the one who will shepherd my people Israel." The idea that this new king could come from Bethlehem had to be a relief to Herod. Jerusalem was an intellectual bastion, a city filled with wealthy elites and dignitaries, like London, or New York City, or Hong Kong. Bethlehem, on the other hand, was a rural town filled with farmers and shepherds. The difference between the two was like the difference between Paris, France, and Paris, Texas. Herod must have reasoned that any king born in Bethlehem could not pose a serious threat. If this prophecy were true, this child would be a peasant king; he might be distracting with his populist message or at worst foment a revolt, but he wasn't a real threat. He would be no match for Herod's army. Satisfied with their answer, Herod released the chief priests from his court.

Herod then secretly called for the astrologers. He wanted to know exactly when the star appeared, how they came to connect it with Jerusalem, and what they thought the prophecy meant. When he had their answers, Herod told them that his Jewish advisors had found their mistake, and that the child was in a town called Bethlehem, as told in a prophecy from one of the Jewish sacred texts. Of course, Herod didn't pass on this information because he suddenly developed a streak of altruism. I imagine he even doubted that the prophecy could be true, but if it somehow *was* true, he needed to keep an eye on the situation. He asked the astrologers to let him know if they found this child king, because he wanted to worship him also. The astrologers didn't buy that any more than we do, so after they left Bethlehem, they traveled home by another way and avoided Herod altogether. Tragically, however, Herod's proactive paranoia eventually led him to murder every boy under the age of two in the surrounding areas. He wasn't the kind of guy who took chances.

After the astrologers left Herod's court, they journeyed ten miles south of Jerusalem to the humble little town of Bethlehem, following the star. At long last, they came to the door of the house of Mary and Joseph. They dismounted their tired camels and took out the gifts that had traveled so far to be given to an unknown king. I cannot imagine what a surprise it must have been for whoever was on the other side of that door. These foreign men, these very un-Jewish, pagan astrologers so determined to see her child and offer him gifts of gold, frankincense, and myrrh was likely yet another portrait Mary would treasure and ponder in her heart for years to come.

As the astrologers made their way toward the Christ child, it didn't matter that this was not their homeland or their native religion. In that moment, they realized and proclaimed that this was their king.

# AN EXPANSIVE KINGDOM

Epiphany is the day in the Christian calendar year when we celebrate that a group of pagan astrologers claimed a Jewish child as their king. *Epiphany* is a fitting word for it, because it describes when something rather surprising and delightful happens or is discovered. When the astrologers saw the eastern star and followed the twists and turns all the way to Bethlehem, they experienced an epiphany. Beyond all human understanding or expectation, they became players in the unfolding story of the God of Abraham and Sarah. Epiphany is the declaration that God is not just God of the Israelites but God of foreign pagan astrologers, too. Though God's activity in the world began with one family, Jesus' kingship begins with one world. Christ's birth marks the beginning of the promised Kingdom of God on earth. And that

Kingdom, as we see in Epiphany, reaches far beyond Jerusalem.

From the very beginning of Jesus' life on earth, God makes it clear this Messiah is going to muddy the lines between who is in and who is out. The story of the astrologers is the story of God's expanding love from the viewpoint of unexpected outsiders.

> This Messiah is going to muddy the lines between who is in and who is out.

This outward-bound trajectory is heralded by a couple of insiders as well: two devout Jewish people living in Jerusalem named Simeon and Anna.

The Gospel of Luke tells us that Simeon was a devout man who had the presence of God's Spirit resting on him. Simeon was given the promise that he would not pass away until he saw the coming Messiah. One day, Simeon felt the overwhelming urge to go to the Temple. It happened to be the day Mary and Joseph brought Jesus to be circumcised, a custom under Mosaic Law. The Scriptures tell us that when Simeon saw the baby, his heart leaped within him and he realized this was the infant face of the Messiah. He rushed toward Mary, hands outstretched.

If I ever saw a strange man rushing toward me, overly eager to hold my baby, there is absolutely *no way* I would comply—but Mary did. I wonder if somehow

Mary could see that Simeon knew in his heart what she knew in hers. This was not just any baby—this was the Messiah. Simeon took Jesus into his arms as he raised his face and said, "God, now I can go in peace, because my eyes have finally seen your salvation—a light given to all people, both inside Israel and out."

All who were gathered in the Temple must have been perplexed. It was strange enough that Simeon rushed to grab the baby of an unknown woman, but his declaration was stranger still. A light for people outside of Israel? What would someone outside of Israel have to do with a Jewish prophecy in which they did not even believe? Simeon began to open up for those in the Temple the radical and unknown idea that "Messiah" may not be a regional or solely Hebrew title. Plenty of prophecies described the Messiah as having an effect on the entire world, but most people probably assumed it was hyperbole. Nobody actually thought it would *happen* until word spread of a group of astrologers from the East who came to pay homage to a Jewish king; and until Simeon made somewhat of a scene that day in the Temple.

The commotion in the Temple on the day Jesus was circumcised did not end with Simeon, however. After Simeon's words of blessing, an eighty-four-year-old woman made her way through the crowd toward Mary and Joseph, her voice raised as she uttered praises to God, grabbing the arms of those near her as she announced this baby would fulfill God's promise of a coming king. It was Anna, a well-known widow in the Temple. She never left, day or night, but always stayed in the courts, fasting and praying. It is hard to say what people thought of Anna, whether they disapproved of her eccentricities as a widowed woman in a Temple full of men, refusing to leave long after all of them went home. But Anna, like Simeon, had a personal stake in this child. Day after day she prayed for the Messiah to come, and if this was the child promised, she wanted to tell every person in the Temple who would listen.

Simeon and Anna were children of Abraham and Sarah, descendants of God's great covenant. The Scriptures declaring the coming Messiah were familiar words and phrases they carried in their hearts, that when spun together brought to life the portrait of God's promised king like a flipbook. Even though the promise of God was changing to expand previously excluded people, Simeon and Anna could see the future of God unfolding before their eyes. Simeon and Anna announced to the people in the Temple that day that this was not business as usual. Something remarkable was breaking forth in the cries of this baby, activating yet another crescendo in God's

God's good news is not just good news for the children of Abraham and Sarah. It is good news for everyone.

coming promise as God's unfolding story expanded to
include the whole world. God's good news is not just
good news for the children of Abraham and Sarah.
It is good news for everyone.

The prophetic voices of Simeon and Anna are
significant because they bring the life of Jesus into its
rightful context. God may be slowly revealing that God's
good news travels vastly beyond national or religious
borders, but the importance of this news can only be
understood in the context of its beginning as a single
promise. Simeon and Anna hold on to that promise,
the one given to the family of Abraham and Sarah, the
promise that God would make them a great nation
through whom all the other families on earth would
be blessed. This promise is the catalyst by which all
the other dominoes tumble, clicking from generation
to generation, continuing even now. Simeon and Anna
raised their voices in the Temple because they saw God's
new future approaching.

## THE GREAT BANQUET FEAST

From the way his story begins, we quickly get the feeling that Jesus is not likely to reinforce the status quo.
The arrival of a group of pagan astrologers on Jesus'
doorstep foreshadows a pattern of Jesus bringing

in—and reaching out toward—people on the margins. Jesus evidenced this many times in his life. He spoke to prostitutes, touched lepers, had dinner with tax collectors, rubbed elbows with adulterers. In addition to his actions, which showed a life committed to people on the fringes, he also enjoyed telling stories to reinforce his point. Jesus told stories about sibling rivalry and forgiveness, about laborers who worked less than others and got paid equally. He also told a story about a banquet . . . while at a banquet.

One evening, Jesus was having dinner with some Pharisees, hosted at the home of a well-known leader. People were watching Jesus, waiting to see what he was going to do. Those who didn't like Pharisees thought less of Jesus for being seen with them. Some of the Pharisees themselves were perplexed, because they were very familiar with the harsh words he often had for their behavior. Everyone seemed eager to see how the evening would develop. It was like people watching a hockey game, waiting for a fight to break out. But Jesus did not throw a punch. Instead, he told a story.

Once, he told them, someone gave a great banquet and invited many people. When it was time, the host sent his servants to remind those who had been invited, but they all began to make excuses. One said, "I just bought some property and I need to go take a look at it." Another said, "I just made some investments, and I need to go talk with my broker." Another said, "I just got married and I need to be home with my spouse." The servant returned to the host and reported that nobody was coming. Then the host said, "Go out into the streets and into town and bring in the poor, the disabled, the forgotten people." So the servant did, and he returned with a sizable crowd. But there was still more room at the table, so the host said, "Go back out there! Head out into the roads, and invite anyone you see to come in for a delicious feast. Let's fill up every spot at the table because none of the people I invited plan to show up."

At Epiphany, uninvited guests showed up at the feet of Jesus with gifts, while many who were invited did not bother to come. The Temple authorities did not follow the astrologers on their journey to Bethlehem. The people who had met the foreign sages on the streets of Jerusalem did not feel compelled to go and see for themselves. None of those who were invited came to the banquet feast. They continued life as usual, busy as they were with duties, and jobs, and family obligations. God stirred in an unexpected place, a place far in the East where a group of astrologers were gazing at the same stars Abraham and Sarah were promised their descendants would outnumber. And they came.

The guests in Jesus' parable were not required to show birth certificates confirming membership in the twelve tribes or take a religious knowledge quiz or write out some sort of statement of belief. If they wanted to come to the feast, the host had a spot waiting for them.

I fear the institutional Christian church has too often attempted to write up the guest list to a party where they ought to be thankful to be honored guests. We are not the hosts of Jesus' kingdom party. Just like everyone else, we are invited simply to come and take a seat at the table.

My community of faith is filled with people who have experienced being removed from the guest list, or refused at the door, forced out by people who have taken over Jesus' hosting duties. They began to question something, so they were not able to be "in fellowship" with church members anymore. They suffered health problems that were seen as an unwelcome burden on the "needs and requirements of church ministry," so they were let go. They questioned why the advertising budget was vastly disproportionate to the money spent feeding people, and they were told to get behind the "vision" of the church or to leave. They were simply not deemed good enough.

I cannot imagine what Jesus will say about such things.

We are not the hosts of God's dinner party. We do not make up the invite list or determine the menu. We are honored guests. Jesus is very

We are not the hosts of God's dinner party. We are honored guests.

clear with us—if we cannot come to the banquet with
those on the outside—the poor, the disabled, the forgotten
and marginalized, the astrologer, the prostitute, the tax
collector, the Pharisee—our place at the dinner table will
be filled by someone else.

Just before Jesus told this parable, he said those
who assume they have a place of honor at God's table
may be surprised to find they are turned away at the
door. They wanted the feast but were not willing to
believe in the promise. The promise is not an invitation
to an exclusive party. The promise, in Jesus' words, is
a feast where people from all walks of life gather from
east, west, north, and south to eat joyfully together at
God's table. We say these words of Jesus often at Journey
before we take communion. It reminds us that we are
part of God's promise, but it also reminds us that the
promise is not ours alone. Christ's table of communion
is not our table, and any who want to come and be part
of God's feast are invited. It is not our duty to turn people away, because it is not our table. We, like everyone
else, are Jesus' honored guests.

Epiphany celebrates the God who unites us from
east and west, north and south. I have seen in my own
family how God has united a mother and father from
cultures, families, and religions that were worlds apart.
In that most surprising joining together, the trajectory
of our family has been brought into the expanding

promise of God. My parents leave out a number of wise men (and their camels) year-round, perched in their colorful robes. Even now as I walk through the halls of my parents' home, I pause to reflect on their presence in this house of converts. My mother, a Lebanese Druze, traveled a great distance to find the path of Jesus, and these wise men act as signatories to that crucial part of our family history where foreigners and outsiders are welcomed as family members. In more ways than I can ever explain, the celebration of Epiphany is our story. It is the strange and wonderful trip into the heart of God from a world that felt millions of miles away.

Paul wrote in his letter to the Ephesian church that we were once strangers and aliens to the promise of God. We had no idea this promise was our promise, this God our God. But Jesus has proclaimed peace to those of us who were far off and peace to those who were near. We are no longer strangers, but members of the family of God. And we are being built together, brick by brick, shoulder to shoulder, into a dwelling place for God. We are being fashioned into one humanity through the body of the child king who began bringing together people from far and near as soon as he got here.

This act of bringing together and building together is what Jesus has called us to do as well. We come from various places with different histories and legacies and life stories, and a spectrum of gifts. But all of these come together under the epiphany that is the Christ child, this infant who joins our myriad bricks together and fashions them into a home.

God brings peace to those who are far off and peace to those who are near. This is the very definition of good news. It is why God created the world, why Jesus was compelled to live and die and be resurrected among us, why the Spirit moves even now, breathing peace into those spaces that lie between. In Jesus the whole structure of the world is growing together, forming a new kind of temple, a dwelling place for all to call home.

# 4

# From Gatekeepers to Door Openers

look ridiculous in a priest collar—those white plastic round things usually worn with black shirts. Some of my colleagues look almost regal in them, or at the very least professional. I look like an eight-year-old playing dress-up in my Catholic uncle's closet. Once I had to wear the collar underneath a long black robe with a white cord belt around the waist when I officiated at a friend's wedding. I felt like shouting, "Make way for the hobbit monk!" as I schlumped down the aisle. Thankfully, I don't have to wear these accouterments often. However, when I was a chaplain at a retirement community, that black shirt and white collar was my uniform because if I didn't wear it, I was mistaken for a teenage candy striper.

When you work as a chaplain to Alzheimer's patients, not giving the right signal about who you are is quite problematic. It's difficult to convince residents to let you pray for them or talk with them about anything of substance when they assume you are fulfilling a service-hour quotient to remain on the cheerleading squad. My chaplain friend Robin finally sat me down and said, "Honey, it's time to call in the big guns. We need to get you a collar."

A few weeks later, I quite apprehensively headed into work, black leather Book of Common Prayer in hand and white plastic collar around my neck, thinking surely someone would remind me it was not Halloween and I could give up the act. When I made my rounds, however, I was completely taken aback at the difference it made. Residents recognized my purpose, and even my face. I was invited to pray for family members; residents told me stories of their religious experiences growing up; fewer of them fell asleep during my sermon at our weekly chapel service.

The greatest difference came when I visited Mrs. Williams. On my very first day on the job there—jolly and naïve, wearing my nondescript civilian clothes—I bounded down the hallway ready to make these people my new best friends. I moseyed into Mrs. Williams's room all smiley and pastoral, ready for another positive encounter when, before I could even get out a hello, she twirled around in her wheelchair and cursed me out at the top of

her lungs. "Who the hell are you?" she bellowed. "*Get out!*"
I stood there motionless, gawking in disbelief, until she
charged at me again and almost ran over my feet. The next
time I visited, I came in with less of my normal verve,
speaking in quieter tones, aiming for what Robin called
a "calming presence." After my first attempt at a gentle,
calming hello, Mrs. Williams glared at me and yelled,
"*What?* Speak up! I can hardly hear you!" I raised my
voice a little, to normal speaking tones. Her glare began
to get very serious as again she yelled, "*What?*" Smiling
tentatively, I turned up my volume one last time and she
roared, "I'm not *deaf.* You don't have to *yell at me.* Geeze!"

So much for calming presence.

One time, Mrs. Williams even came busting into
the room next door during a nice visit I was having
with her neighbor and made such a racket I was forced
to leave to deescalate the situation. It apparently wasn't
enough to throw me out of her room. She wanted me
ejected from the building. Mrs. Williams became my
biggest challenge, and I was determined to turn the
tide. I knew we wouldn't become best friends, but I was
hoping at the very least she would not explode when
she saw me coming down the hallway. The day I first
wore my collar, I made my way down the hallway until I
found myself again at the doorway of doom. I muttered
a little prayer, took a deep breath, and stepped inside.
At first, she jolted her head up, ready to pounce on the

unassuming person who had wandered into her lair. I braced myself. But in an instant, her face relaxed, and I dare say she smiled. "Oh," she said. "Hello."

Hello?

I was almost too shocked to respond, but I grabbed that sliver of opportunity like it was my last piece of bread, and I cautiously sat down beside her. "How are you today, Mrs. Williams?" And just like that, we began the first of many pleasant visits. She told me about her favorite psalm (which I read to her on every subsequent visit), about her sons and how they fought in the war, about the little church she attended with her grandmother as a girl. To my great surprise, Mrs. Williams and I became friends, all because of a little white piece of plastic.

## THE GOD SQUAD

There is a long tradition of religious people wearing clothes that signify their purpose. Certain clothes have a way of calling up an idea about a person, of instructing you in how to address someone, whether that means telling them you would like a grande chai latte or prayer for your ailing parent. Titles do the same thing, in a less obtrusive sort of way. Titles and uniforms act as signals, directing us across the walkways of one another's positions in life in hopes of avoiding chaos.

In the story of God, titles tend to come about with
a lot of history. This is certainly true of the title "priest."

The first priest mentioned in
the Bible is a very strange fellow named Melchizedek. When
I say he was a strange fellow, I
mean it. Ancient sources of the
time speak of him as if he were
some sort of heavenly being, and the New Testament
letter Hebrews describes him as having no beginning
or end, and no parents. The one story we have about
Melchizedek comes from Genesis. Abraham had just
finished rescuing his rascally cousin Lot from a tyrannical king and Melchizedek was leading the charge to
welcome him home at his return. When Abraham saw
Melchizedek, he offered him a portion of his war spoils,
and Melchizedek blessed him. This is strange, because
both offering gifts and receiving a blessing from someone were signs of deferring authority, and as you know,
we are not used to seeing Abraham defer to anybody,
much less to a stranger. The story has no commentary
on this; it merely describes Melchizedek as "Priest of the
Most High God," so we assume that must mean something . . . although we really don't know what, or where
he came from, or why he arrived out of nowhere just
then, or what he was wearing that signaled his status. It's
odd, isn't it, that the first priest mentioned in the Bible

**In the story of God, titles
tend to come about with
a lot of history.**

makes a cameo appearance rather than being a series regular? We'll get back to this story in a minute.

The next time we encounter the title "priest" is in relation to Moses' father-in-law, Jethro. Jethro came to visit Moses and the newly freed Israelites after they left Egypt, and Moses told him all about what happened— the plagues, how Pharaoh stubbornly wouldn't let the people go, how they almost got killed near the Red Sea before it parted in two and they ran across to freedom. After hearing all of this, Jethro got up and praised God for clearing a way to freedom for the Israelites.

The next day Jethro watched as Moses toiled away at the arduous task of leading these people. Not only was Moses trying to keep their spirits high and keep them moving in the right direction, he was also spending an inordinate amount of time mediating between arguing parties. Jethro watched him listen to case after case from morning until night. Sounding a little like a nature explorer trying to make sense of a strange animal ritual, Jethro pulled Moses aside and asked, "What is this thing you're doing with the people? Why are they standing before you all day?" And Moses said, "Because when people have an issue, they come to me and I help them sort it out." Jethro replied, "Moses, if you keep this up, you are going to wear yourself out. Listen—you're going to have to teach these people to know the way and walk it. Bring in more leaders, let them settle most

of these matters themselves and only come to you for
the big stuff." Moses, who was likely exhausted from the
burden and desperate to try something more sustainable,
took Jethro's words to heart and did what he said. (Most
American pastors could use a Jethro, too.)

Soon after that, God called Moses up to Mount
Sinai. God told Moses to tell the Israelites, "All of you
know what I have done in Egypt, how I have carried
you on eagle's wings and brought you close to me.
Though all creation is mine, you are my people, and
if you will follow me, you will be a tribe of priests
and a holy nation." Moses repeated these words to the
Israelites who gathered to hear, and they all agreed that
was what they would do—they would follow God and
live like a tribe of priests.

This was quite a change. If anything, up to this
point Moses had been giving a good go at being something like a "king priest," head of the God Squad, the
one guy in charge of everything while everyone else
mindlessly followed along. Jethro, the one with the actual
title of priest, had to come in and point out that this
was not the way to go. Moses would be exhausted and
the people would never learn how to walk toward God's
horizon. That wasn't freedom—or faithfulness—for anybody. God hadn't told them to be a tribe with priests, but
a tribe of priests. All of them were called to walk toward
God's promised horizon.

For a while, things went more smoothly, as everyone began to pitch in. But before long Moses was carrying the lion's share of the burden again. He complained to God, and God responded by making Moses' brother Aaron, and Aaron's sons, into priests. This is how the tradition of priests in the Bible officially began. For every generation that followed, the descendants of Aaron would take up the title and responsibility from the generation before. From the beginning, priests were meant to be examples for the rest of the Israelites, showing them what it looks like to follow God's path. They were not meant to be stand-ins for the faithfulness of everyone else, but conduits that pushed everyone toward the outward movement of God.

## CURTAIN CALL

When the Israelites finally settled in Jerusalem and built their Temple, the role of High Priest emerged. High Priests did exactly what you'd guess—they were the priests over all the other priests, the ones at the top of the religious food chain, the heads of the God Squad. The most important duty of the year came on Yom Kippur, the Day of Atonement. On that day, the High Priest would pull back a thick curtain that measured sixty feet high, thirty feet wide, and four inches thick to enter the Holy of Holies, the innermost court of the Temple where the presence of God was said to dwell. The High Priest then made an offering to God on behalf of the entire nation to ask forgiveness from God for all the wrongdoings incurred over the past year.

The Gospels of Matthew, Mark, and Luke tell us that when Jesus died on a Friday, the thick velvet curtain that separated the presence of God from the rest of the Temple (and, by extension, the world) was torn in two from top to bottom. In Jesus, the boundary that stood between the presence of God and the rest of the world was permanently shattered. God's presence has come to those of us standing out in the courts and on the streets, blemished and wearing civilian clothes. We don't need a priest or a holy press pass to be near God, because God has come to us.

One of the many names for Jesus is Emmanuel, which means God-with-us. When the curtain tore in two, God performed a dramatic exit from the Holy of Holies to signal to all of us that being God-with-us was more than just a name. It was a promise. God has chosen to be with us and has invited all of us into the innermost courts of God's presence. In Jesus, God reminds us that God has not promised to be God distant from us, God sequestered from us, even God of the sufficiently religious. God promises to be God with us, no matter where we're standing.

That brings us back to the mystery man, Melchizedek. In the New Testament letter of Hebrews, the author brings up Melchizedek's name multiple times in relation to Jesus, repeating again and again that Jesus is a High Priest "in the order of Melchizedek." What in the world does Melchizedek have to do with Jesus? Well, remember how Melchizedek is described—he was a person without beginning or end, without parents, without genealogy. Those last two describe him as someone who walks outside the realms of normal cultural entitlement. What credentials do you hold without a good family name? How do you claim your position in the good old boys' network without them? I don't know what the descriptors about genealogy or family literally mean, but symbolically, they mean that Melchizedek was a person who stood on the fringes, far outside the established norms. They mean his authority does not come from the kind of power channels we humans create.

Jesus was like that too. Irish writer and pastor Pete Rollins mentions the irony of Matthew (the Gospel writer) painstakingly describing Jesus' family genealogy, only to hit the punch line at the end that Jesus is not actually connected to it, because he is not descended of Joseph but the Holy Spirit. Jesus was not really one to navigate culturally sanctioned power channels; on the contrary, he seemed to delight in subverting them. You can tell that just by looking at the disciples, whose shelves were lined with fishing gear rather than framed academic or religious degrees.

Like Matthew, the writer of Hebrews goes to great lengths over a number of chapters to describe Jesus as our final High Priest only to hit the punch line that Jesus wasn't actually qualified for the job of priest to begin with. In Jewish tradition, you had to be a descendant of Aaron, the first priest, and a member of his tribe, the Levites, and Jesus was neither. And that doesn't begin to mention all the other reasons Jesus was unqualified by performing a slew of unpriestly deeds like touching people considered unclean, touching dead bodies, and breaking Sabbath laws. Jesus tore the curtain open for us because he refused to live in the system of human power. He pointed toward God's horizon instead, which is significantly broader than pedigrees and educational status. After fulfilling the role of High Priest permanently, Jesus immediately disbanded the power network altogether.

The letter of Hebrews says that the regulations of the priesthood didn't work, but in Jesus we have a better hope, a bigger promise, that draws us nearer to God. God wants to write these promises in our minds and on our hearts, so that everyone will know God. Let's hold on tight to our hope and spur each other on toward love, the letter continues, because God has opened up a new and living way for us, and we know God's promise is faithful.

We have our permanent power-subverting High Priest—it's now time for us to focus once again on being the priesthood.

## PRIESTHOOD OF ALL OR PRIESTHOOD OF A FEW?

God told the Israelites they were to be a tribe of priests all the way back in Exodus 19, and many chapters later in God's story, Jesus echoed the sentiment. God's people are called to be a community of people who help others have a relationship with God. We aren't allowed to hide behind the fancy robes of those who seem to get this more easily than we do. We can't wait for the professionals to arrive. God has imprinted this hopeful horizon on our hearts and in our minds so that all of us can follow God.

During the Protestant Reformation in the 1500s, Martin Luther attempted to address what he believed to be errors within the Christian religious institution of his day. Back then only priests had access to Bibles, and

Luther believed every person had a right to own and read one. He also thought it would be helpful to have some Bibles that were not written in Latin but in a language people could read. He believed this so strongly that he personally began translating the Bible from Latin into his native German to make it available. Luther thought everyday people—not just priests—should be able to serve in the church. All of these ideas led him to coin the phrase "priesthood of all believers," which was one of the central concepts during the evolution of what became Protestantism.

This idea did not come entirely to fruition in practice. Five hundred years have passed since then, but most churches still hold to a list of ministry requirements that look far too similar to the old priesthood system Jesus rather dramatically abolished. Many of my colleagues (ordained colleagues, particularly) disagree with me when I say this feels like bait and switch. Priesthood of all believers! Set down that communion cup unless you have an ordination degree! Doesn't this fall a little short of the priesthood concept we were moving toward? If Jesus is our final High Priest and has made a way for us all to be in God's presence, why are some of us still standing in between?

Questioning a rigid system of requirements for ministers isn't meant to imply we are capable of living faithfully on our own, without anyone (minister or otherwise) to help or guide us. In our American culture, many seem to have taken this phrase "priesthood of all believers" and imbued it with Western individualism, as if Luther's idea means sitting alone in your bedroom reading the Bible and praying to God under your breath, with no need of any outside contact whatsoever. If you had a pantry stocked with canned goods and a can opener, you might be able to stay there indefinitely. This story has never been about walking your own road, but about walking with others toward God's horizon. Both the priest who stands above you and the person who stands isolated from you are being less than faithful to living into God's call to be a tribe of priests.

There is significant distinction between the idea of every person serving as a priest and that of a collective priesthood. Jesus as High Priest does not make us all into simply priests with a lowercase p. We are called and summoned by God not to be priests but to be a priesthood. In fact, the Greek word for priesthood, *hierateuma*, can't even be translated in the singular. A person cannot be described as "a *hierateuma*" because the word can only be used as a collective term. If you told someone you bought a pack of gum when really, you only got a single gumball, you would be misleading them, if not flat out

> We are called and summoned by God not to be priests but to be a priesthood.

lying. When you say "pack," everybody knows there has to be more than one of them. You can have a four-pack or a six-pack or a twelve-pack but nobody ever buys a one-pack. A *hierateuma* is a pack. You get Jesus, you're part of the priesthood. It's a package deal.

Remember in Exodus 19 when Moses told the Israelites God would make them into a tribe of priests? In 1 Peter 2:9, we hear words similar to those in Exodus 19, but this time, we can hear words of progress. The author writes now not in the language of promise (I will make you a tribe of priests), but with words of fulfillment (You *are* a priesthood). We're not biding our time waiting for the day we get the go-ahead to act like the priesthood pack. We're supposed to be doing that right now. We are called to be a priesthood, that is, a pack of people who seek to follow Jesus faithfully together in the world.

## POINTING TO THE OPEN DOOR

Priests were meant not to work alone but to serve and encourage others. Somewhere along the way they began serving as gatekeepers, those who stood as buffers between God and the rest of us, doling out religious goods and services to those deemed worthy. Institutional religion has always been quite good at this. It seems there are plenty of creative ways to stand at the gate and choose who comes in and out. You can use doctrinal statements, make people sign declarations, ask people to jump through hoops to become members, require strict codes of conduct—the list goes on and on. But Jesus did not act as a gatekeeper or call himself a gatekeeper. He did, however, call himself a gate.

In the Gospel of John, Jesus describes himself as the gate through whom sheep pass to find safe pasture and abundant life. He doesn't describe himself as a gate (or in some translations, a door) because he wants to keep people out. He is the door because he wants to provide a way in. And once this door is open, people can come in and go out and find a good spot on the grass. When the curtain tore in two, Jesus was letting all of us know that the door into God's presence was permanently open. Jesus shows us that a faithful priest is not a gatekeeper but a door opener.

Jesus shows us that a faithful priest is not a gatekeeper but a door opener.

What if we tried to do the same? What if, instead of the inordinate amount of energy and time spent gatekeeping, we spent that time dreaming up every way possible to show people the open door? If we live as gatekeepers, our desire is not to provide a way in or out but to prevent entrance or exit. Gatekeepers determine who is allowed to enter and often proceed to tell others the reason why they do not belong inside. It may be an act of spiritual discipline to remind ourselves that Jesus wouldn't necessarily approve our gatekeeping. We once drew the circle of holiness as a very, very small one. Jesus stood inside it once and for all and promptly took away our penchant for chalk. It's best not to try to take it back from him.

We don't have to create the door for anyone. Jesus has already propped it open. But we can try our best to be people who point to the door, usher people through it, welcome people walking into it. And why wouldn't we? There is life there, and not just any life but life abundant, a good cozy spot on the grass. We wouldn't have much to say if we were inviting people through a door that led to a laundry list of dead regulations. "Come on in! Now please show proper documentation, family name, head over there to get your hair cut and only talk to these pre-approved people." The door doesn't lead to some Orwellian universe. It leads to that space in which we find life beautiful, and meaningful, and real; the space where reconciliation happens; the space where our horizons expand and our hope increases. As followers of Jesus, we are not asked to live as gatekeeping priests, but a community of people who, together, seek to open up a way for others to have a relationship with God alongside us.

We are people who point to that space that is most life
giving.

For Mrs. Williams, that white piece of plastic
opened up a door. It gave her permission to have a relationship not only with me but to share with me her
relationship with God. The question is, did it give her
permission because I happened to have a degree from
seminary and church accreditation, or because it allowed
me to sit beside her as we both faced the open door we
held in common? In the context of a retirement community, my collar and title encouraged the residents to
talk with me about spiritual matters. It provided a visible
signpost through the door. Holding a noticeable position
of spiritual leadership can invite others into dialogue
with the questions and discussions that matter most.
It becomes problematic only when the sanctity of the
position becomes more important than the discussions
it is meant to create.

A friend of mine, Erin, serves as a chaplain in a
children's hospital, and she was once asked to provide
communion to a patient and her family. She had become
a friendly and familiar face to the girl during their many
visits, so it only made sense that they wanted Erin to
serve them and not a stranger. Unfortunately, Erin
was not allowed. Despite being a seminary graduate, she
had not yet finished the long process of ordination to
afford her the "right" to serve communion. It seems not

only consistent to the life of Jesus but just plain common sense to release anyone to offer spiritual nourishment to a family that is hurting. Our world is so full of hurt, we could use all the willing hands we can get. If you want to give time and energy to being spiritually present to someone, whether a friend, work colleague, or a family struggling with illness, I believe the church should encourage and equip you in every possible way. If someone asks us to help them walk toward God's future, don't you think God wants us to help them go?

We can be door openers in plenty of creative ways. If we're honest, we all have had times when we could use some help finding an open door. Jesus invites us to walk this life together as a pack for this very reason.

There have been a number of times when members of Journey have come to a place in the road where faith was not easy, where God felt distant or absent or indifferent. There have been times when the world has felt hostile and cold. There have been times of unspeakable tragedy, times when tears have outnumbered moments of laughter with such proportion that our hearts could hardly bear the weight. In those times, we know we cannot "fix" things for those who are hurting. No easy words will do. We cannot change the sadness for them, or rush them through their grief, or convince them that the sun will rise again tomorrow. So instead, we tell them with all the love we can muster that if they cannot hold their faith for a while, we will hold it for them. They can be cradled in that holy place where Christ has made a way where there was no way, and we will place our hands upon the small of their backs as meager offerings to the great love of Jesus that suspends them, and we will wait until they find their feet again. If they cannot walk through the door just then, we will carry them until they can.

This is what it means to be the priesthood. It means doing everything we can to be good and faithful companions on the journey, side by side, hand in hand. We no longer hold the burden of being priests. We have the honor of living as a priesthood.

## ——— 5 ———

# When the End Is Just the Beginning

During the last week of Jesus' life, the disciples watched as he was betrayed, condemned, beaten, and crucified. Mostly, they watched from a distance. They fell asleep while he prayed fervently in the Garden of Gethsemane. They scattered like mice when he was arrested soon after. Peter, who had followed Jesus at a safe distance as he was taken to the court of the High Priest, denied he knew Jesus three times. Just like that, all twelve of the disciples vanished. The men who were called and taught and loved by Jesus every day for three straight years abandoned him. Just. Like. That.

But the women stayed. Scripture does not tell us how they heard of Jesus' trial, or when they arrived. But when he was suffering upon the cross and breathed his last, they were there. The women who were called and taught and loved by Jesus over the previous three years stood by him, right to the bitter end. All those hopes in Jesus being the Promised One, all that faith in a new horizon had been nailed to a cross with their friend Jesus. They sat at his feet and they wept.

Early the next day, after what was likely a long, arduous night, some of the women awoke and gathered spices to take to Jesus' tomb. They planned to prepare his body for proper burial. Perhaps they were trying to find something to do after a day when they had been rendered so helpless. Perhaps they wanted to find a way to make something right after a day when everything seemed to have gone so wrong. As they approached the tomb, they encountered something world shattering. They found an empty tomb and a risen and very much alive Jesus. Understandably, the women were discombobulated by such a cosmic turn of events. They ran to tell Jesus' disciples, just as Jesus told them to do.

The disciples were equally morose that morning, with good reason. All that time spent with Jesus, all that hope and excitement came crashing down in the worst possible way. They were sitting together, facing the biggest brick wall they had ever encountered. What would they do now? What did this mean? Where would they go from here? What had *happened?* Then the women burst in, likely out of breath and visibly shaken, announcing that the tomb was empty, and Jesus was alive—somehow different, but most definitely alive. The disciples probably looked at their faces and assumed this was a tragic response to the grief they were all experiencing so deeply. They likely looked upon these first witnesses with hearts full of love and heads full of skepticism. How could they reconcile this breathless announcement that Jesus was alive with that massive brick wall with the ominous and conclusive word "*Death*" sprawled across it? Most of the disciples sided with the brick wall until they saw Jesus for themselves, and I can't say as I blame them. Until now, death had always been a sure bet. It just so happened that this moment required them to imagine a new horizon.

At the empty tomb we encounter the One who has defeated that which we believed undefeatable. Death, life's most stringent boundary, has been broken. The solemn finality of human life has been upended by new possibilities, an eternal ellipsis tapping its three little feet into an entirely new kind of future.

Can you imagine? Not "Death" but "Death . . ."

When the women found the empty tomb, they discovered something that would redefine the future for all of us. What we thought was closed and finished now stands open ended, and God only knows what will happen next.

When Jesus appeared to the disciples, the companions who had deserted him in his most desperate time of need, he greeted them saying, "Peace be with you." He talked with them, ate fish with them, and even invited one of them to stick his fingers in Jesus' wounds, just to be sure. And Jesus once again spoke the command God has been repeating since the very beginning of this story: go. Go tell the whole world what has happened! No matter how traumatic the experience of the crucifixion had been, no matter how astonishing the presence of Jesus now was, they were called to go. God was still on the move, and God's people were called to march jubilantly behind the ellipsis of God's new future, declaring good news to all creation. It was time to leave behind their fear of the permanence of death. Jesus asks us to follow the resurrection radiance that has debuted smack-dab in the middle of human history, the glow of God's future flung like processional rose petals along our path.

## GETTING OUR LIVES BACK

Generally speaking, the phrase "eternal life" often conjures up visions of a fountain of youth or the immortality of the Greek gods—but Easter doesn't speak to us in these general terms. The empty tomb specifically announces our invitation into God's eternal life, which is not a morning-after-death pill or a cup of magical water to dissolve our wrinkles. It certainly isn't a get-out-of-jail-free card

or a train ticket out of the world God is redeeming. Those
might sound like nice horizons, but they're pretty selfish
ones, and they have little to do with the vast expanse of
open sky that stands outside of Jesus' empty tomb. Easter
doesn't trivialize our lives—it revitalizes them, reorients
them, makes them even more valuable and beautiful.
Easter reminds us that God takes our lives quite seriously,
calling us to be a community of people set apart to speak
words of life and not death, hope and not despair. If
we're going to take Jesus' boundary-breaking resurrection
seriously, we can't consider our lives (or deaths) cursory
or unimportant.

Easter doesn't change the fact that all of us will
die, and let's be honest, nobody's completely looking
forward to that. I don't know why many Jesus followers have such a hard time acknowledging that death is
sad and often tragic, as if saying out loud that you're
angry about cancer or car accidents somehow makes
you less faithful. Remember when Jesus cried as he
watched Mary and Martha grieve the loss of their brother?
Remember when Jesus was praying in the Garden of
Gethsemane just before Judas turned him in, and he
begged God to take all this pain away? Jesus doesn't ask us
to gloss over the sadness of death, and God never asks
us to choose between Good Friday (the day we remember Jesus' death) and Easter. We remember both, because
only then can we see the fullness of God's horizon.

Death doesn't disappear, but it looks different under Easter's dawning horizon. In baptism, we proclaim that difference by reminding ourselves of this new horizon and restorying the meaning of our own deaths. When John the Baptist stood in the Jordan River calling people to repent because the Kingdom of God was at hand, they would wade into the river until the water came up to their waists. John would plunge them underneath the water and slowly lift them back up. Jewish rituals of purification did something similar to this, but John expanded our idea of repentance to include not only cleansing but, more radically, total rebirth. In baptism we choose to come symbolically face to face with our own pending death. We concede our own mortality, succumb to it as the water closes over our heads, so that we may rise up in hope and leave our fear of death's finality under the surface. As my pastor declared when I was baptized, we are buried with Jesus in baptism and raised to walk with him in the newness of life. We symbolically die so that we can literally live like people who will be resurrected.

When we follow Easter's horizon, we decide to embrace life and reject all that stands in the way of us living the abundant life we've been given, both in our individual lives as well as our collective ones. Injustice, torture, greed, political expediency, pride, tyrannical governments, selfishness, retribution, murder—Jesus confronted all of these very real issues (and more) in his own death to show us that we can find a new and living way through them also. These forces are always at work in our world, both within us and within our culture, but resurrection hope keeps us from succumbing to them or allowing them to stand in the way of God's horizon. At Easter, we celebrate that these powers and forces have been rejected as lasting currency in God's world. They have been time-stamped, and there will come a day when they will expire. As those who follow Jesus, we are called to remind these death machines that they are time-stamped. We reject their authority over our lives, our families, and our societies, and we refuse to abide by their rules. We choose to live life not under the oppression of the death machines but under the loving banner of the living God.

This is why charges of anti-Semitism that infiltrate the story of Jesus' death and resurrection represent the worst form of lifeless religion. Those charges are spoken from inside the death machines of racism, of retribution, of alienation and exclusion. Easter has nothing to do with those machines, and those of us who follow the God of life must reject those charges. If the story of Jesus were repeated in America today, those who hurl such charges should humbly consider whether they would not find themselves calling for his execution in the courts as well. As long as we live in a world powered by cultural death machines, the ending to Jesus' story, no matter who plays what part, would remain the same.

Death's claim upon us will not have the last word. The last word will be God's, and it will be a word of life. When God interrupted the history of death with the resurrection of Jesus, God gave all of us the gift of new sight. We can now see the world outside of the constraints of the death machines that choke life out of us and out of our neighbors and see instead the rich soil of God's horizon where abundant life grows. We can imagine, and believe in, a world where death sentences upon divinely created life will be overruled. At Easter, we get our lives back, and we are freed to start truly living.

## UNLIKELY HERALDS OF THE WORLD'S BEST NEWS

The entire story of God is a journey away from the horizon of death and toward the horizon of life. Throughout the story, God uses people on the margins of society, outside of the powerful cultural mechanisms, to declare God's coming Kingdom. Exiled murderers like Moses proclaim God's freedom, pagan astrologers announce

Jesus' reign, and a handful of fishermen become Jesus'
understudies. Elizabeth, the mother of John the Baptist,
is one of the many barren women—Sarah, Rachel,
Hannah—who pop up in the story of God. Though
their society looked down upon them, God looked to
these women to propel the story of God forward. Not
only do these stories reinforce God as one who can
bring life out of emptiness, they also show God as one
who remembers—and calls—those society has know-
ingly overlooked. God didn't come to barren women
just because bringing life out of a barren womb is
miraculous. God came to them because they were
forgotten.

Jesus' life is bracketed by women who lived in a system that routinely undervalued them. Mary was an unwed
pregnant teenager, which, as you can imagine, could not
have been easy. When she rushed to her cousin Elizabeth's
house soon after hearing the news of her pregnancy, the
two of them became the first to celebrate the coming of
the Christ child and ponder what it might mean for the
world. At the end of Jesus' life, Mary Magdalene poured
a jar of scented oil all over Jesus' feet and wiped it with
her hair, a gesture Jesus received as a loving preparation
for his death and burial even as the disciples reprimanded
her. At the cross, the women who had followed Jesus all
the way from Galilee were still by his side. They were
loyal when others forgot him, perhaps because they knew

all too well how he felt. They loved Jesus because Jesus saw them, addressed them, and engaged them. The space Jesus made for them is largely why they found themselves in the garden that Easter morning. Jesus had always honored them; they would see to it that even in death, they would honor Jesus. Little did they know they would be called to be unlikely heralds of the world's best news. It would fall upon their loyal shoulders to declare Jesus' boundary-breaking resurrection to the world.

There was one slight problem. Who was going to take the eyewitness account of grieving women seriously in a culture where women held no legal authority? If the story of God was to continue, people were going to have to believe these previously invisible women's story.

Maybe it's impossible to envision eternal life when you can't even see the worth of the human being standing right in front of you. At Easter, we not only get our lives back. We get our eyes back, too.

## PRACTICING RESURRECTION

Just as we are called to practice being free, we are called to practice resurrection. What does life lived outside the

death machines look like? When Jesus was on his way to
Jerusalem, a lawyer asked him that question. "Teacher,"
he asked, "what do I have to do to inherit eternal life?"
Jesus asked him what the law of God said regarding the
matter. The lawyer answered, "It says that I'm to love
God with all my heart, all my soul, all my strength, and
all my mind; and I'm to love my neighbor as I love
myself." Jesus replied, "Sounds like you already know the
right answer. Do these things, and you will experience
eternal life." But the lawyer wanted to justify himself, so
he asked, "But who is my neighbor?" Jesus responded,
as he often did, with a story.

Once a traveler was going down from Jerusalem
to Jericho and was ambushed by robbers who stripped
him, beat him, and then left him there half-dead. A
priest happened to be going down the same road, and
when the priest saw the traveler, the priest passed over
to the other side of the road and kept walking. A little
while later, a Levite (a Temple assistant) came down the
road and did the same exact thing. But then a Samaritan
came along, and the Samaritan was moved with sym-
pathy when he saw the traveler, and he went over and
tended to the traveler's wounds with great care. Then
the Samaritan brought the traveler to a hotel and continued to take care of him. The next day, the Samaritan
took out two days' worth of wages and gave them to
the hotel manager, saying, "Take care of this person, and

when I come back, I'll repay you for whatever more you spend." "Which one of these people was a neighbor to the man who was beaten?" Jesus asked. The lawyer said, "The one who showed him mercy." Jesus said, "Go and do the same."

When Jesus was asked to give an example of what practicing resurrection looks like, Jesus said it looks like tending to people we find hurting on the road. The Samaritan wasn't going to let theft, violence, and death be the last word for the traveler, so he spoke a word of life instead. That's a worthwhile enough lesson, but Jesus used a Samaritan as the hero of the story for a reason as well. The Samaritans were not highly regarded by their Jewish neighbors. The Samaritans didn't worship at the Temple in Jerusalem because they built their own on Mount Gerizim, so the two groups often fought over which Temple was the central one. Even worse, though, the Samaritans renamed their Temple in honor of the Greek god Zeus after the ruler Antiochus Epiphanies demanded it. This, of course, went against every grain of monotheism in Jewish faith, which led to the Maccabean revolt that is celebrated every year at Hanukkah. After that, Jewish-Samaritan relations quite understandably went downhill. Jesus, of course, was fully aware of the tortured relationship between the two ethnic groups when he told the parable. The crowd gathered was likely ruffled at the mere mention of a

Samaritan, much less the punch line about the Samaritan as the faithful hero to the Law of God. None of Jesus' listeners would expect the Samaritan walking along the road to have the integrity or proper beliefs or fully developed religious sensibility to do the right thing. Through the parable, Jesus doesn't just tell his listeners, "You should have known to stop and help the traveler." Jesus is also telling us, "Sometimes the most faithful person is someone you assumed didn't have the right kind of faith."

A few years ago, I had a conversation with a group of Christian ministers regarding the church's response to extreme poverty. We were hoping to brainstorm ways to address the global problem, because Scripture has more to say about caring for the poor than any other topic— by a long shot. As we discussed joining efforts with a number of nonprofit organizations seeking to combat extreme poverty, one of the ministers asked, "Is this a Christian organization? Because if isn't, my church just won't feel good about supporting them." (The organization in question at that particular moment was not religious in nature.) I asked him to clarify his concerns. He said, "Well, how do we know they are doing it for the right reasons?" Someone responded, "I doubt the mother who needs food for her starving children cares very much about 'right reasons.'" A few of us also gently pointed out that this organization had done more to care for the orphan as Jesus instructed than most churches in our urban metroplexes combined. Perhaps we should ask ourselves if *we* are operating under the right reasons. The honest truth is that this "secular" organization has stopped to help the poor along the road while most churches have passed by the poor without so much as a passing glance, so which of us is practicing resurrection?

Jesus has told us what we must do to experience eternal life, that is, to live life resurrected. We are to love God with all we have and all we are, and love our neighbor as ourselves. We know the right answer. The difficulty comes in living it out. All three of the travelers on the road had understandable excuses for not stopping to help the wounded man. But if we truly desire eternal life, we shouldn't spend our energy looking for loopholes, trying to find ways to justify ourselves as the lawyer did. We should look for ways to be bearers of life to others on every road we find ourselves, no matter what the person in need may look like.

Eternal life is not a ticket we hold but a lifestyle we inhabit. If we follow the resurrected Jesus, we have to practice resurrection. We have to practice continually being advocates of life rather than people resigned to death. We have to do the hard work of disentangling ourselves from

Eternal life is not a ticket we hold but a lifestyle we inhabit.

the death machines, both individually and systemically. Following God requires us to treat people in a way that often bumps up against what is culturally acceptable. Treating others with grace and forgiveness, loving our enemies, and seeking peaceful reconciliation often look quite foreign to a world that seems to reward those who look out for themselves. And unfortunately, our eyes have filters of prejudice, animosity, resentment, fear, and pride. It can be a lot to look through.

Practicing resurrection means seeing the world through the eyes of God as best we can. At Easter, we claim God as the God of life—we boldly shout it in the face of the death machines—because we are convinced it's the best news this world will ever receive.

# 6

# Wind Power

When I was a child, the Petroleum Museum was one of my favorite places to visit around town. The Petroleum Museum is just what you'd expect—a collection of exhibits that describes the history of oil in our region. The museum was filled with interactive exhibits, but my brother and I always knew exactly which one we were hitting first without even saying a word. We would stampede like little rhinos toward the simulated nitroglycerin explosion, positioning our feet on the square platform outlined on the floor and excitedly pushing a big clunky button to begin the video of "Tom the Driller." Tom showed us how he packed tins with nitrogen to send down the oil well hole. Once the tins were in place, Tom would trigger the explosion, which would break up the rocks around the hole and let the oil flow more freely. Tom would flash a big smile and say, "We're about ready to go now. Are you ready?" My brother and I would glance at each other with a mixture of anticipation and excitement as Tom started counting down, "5 . . . 4 . . . 3 . . . 2 . . . 1 . . . ," and *boom!* The floor platform would burst up, popping our feet momentarily off the ground while the sound of the explosion surrounded our senses. Meanwhile Tom the Driller would laugh and holler out, "Ooooh-*wee!*" Our hearts would jump so high when it boomed you would never know we had pushed that button a zillion times. It was fantastic.

After visiting the Petroleum Museum, my brother and I would talk about how we wished our dad worked in the fields like Tom the Driller. Like most people in Midland, Dad worked in oil and gas, but his sales responsibilities kept him safely at a distance from the magical lure of the oil fields. We would have given anything to tell our classmates that he laughed in the face of yesterday's harrowing nitroglycerin explosion just like Tom the Driller. This was our version of a West Texas superhero.

When the oil bust hit in the 1980s, the wildcatter oilman lost a bit of his shine. Hollow-eyed people drifted hauntingly down our neighborhood streets, and every

kid saw the uneasiness in the forced smiles of our
mothers as they asked about our day at the dinner table.
We could hear our dads as they gathered in corners at
parties, talking about how they could no longer put all
their eggs in petroleum's volatile basket.

My dad now works for a diversified energy company. West Texas has a lot of oil, that's for sure. But we
also have wind—lots and lots of free wind. And our flat
horizon, already peppered with the silhouettes of oil
wells, looks almost regal under the elongated twirling
wings of gleaming white wind turbines. Wind power is
a much-needed stabilizing counterforce to the seduc-
tive gamble of underground oil, because no matter how
many times we can push that button in the Petroleum
Museum, real-life oil booms aren't that easy to come by.
Wind, however, is as consistent as breath, and its force in
a region where sandstorms can serve as mini-tornadoes
is powerful, if only we can learn how to channel it.

The move from oil wells to abundant wind energy
is a lot like the outward movement of the Holy Spirit in
the story of God. For much of God's story, the Spirit
of God was as powerfully elusive as underground oil,
sometimes making a dramatic appearance and flowing
freely and other times quietly resting under the surface.
If the Spirit ran dry at a particular location, only
God knew where and with whom it would turn up
next. After Jesus' resurrection, however, the Spirit of

God prepared to make Tom the Driller's nitrogen explosion look as insignificant as one of those black cat firecrackers that pop on sidewalks on the Fourth of July. The explosion of God's Spirit at Pentecost changed everything as God once again pushed the boundaries outward.

## CALLING PEOPLE TO GOD

It's difficult for us to understand the importance of Pentecost's explosion if we don't first look at how the Spirit has operated in God's unfolding story. As Genesis describes, in the beginning the Spirit hovered over the waters of the deep, the unformed world lying still with expectation. The wind of God swept over the face of the waters in a mighty rush, and God spoke light and life into the world. The Spirit of God has always been the force of life breathed out onto the world.

The Spirit of God has always been the force of life breathed out onto the world.

For much of God's story, the Spirit came to rest on select individuals who were given a specific calling by God. High-profile leaders like kings and priests were given the Spirit for the duration of their position and relied on the Spirit to provide wisdom and discernment to lead the people in

God's direction. When their time was finished, the Spirit would leave them and rest upon someone else. (The transfer did not always go smoothly. When King Saul was replaced by a young David, Saul was so distressed he attempted to have David killed, which reminds me of the Chinese proverb "Once you ride a tiger, it is difficult to dismount." Apparently it's not easy transitioning back to civilian life after being seized by God's Spirit.)

Prophets and judges were given the Spirit to summon people back to God's path from whatever road they were wandering. The book of Judges often repeats the refrain, "In those days the Israelites did what was wrong in God's eyes," shorthand to let us know God's people had stopped being faithful to the covenant. Judges and prophets came to the people in the same way Moses did when he presented them with choices of life and death and beseeched them to choose life. The Spirit of God was given to move people back toward faithful living.

When John the Baptist's birth is foretold, the Gospel of Luke says that God's Spirit will be with John even in the womb because John will be the one to prepare the way for the coming Messiah. Not surprisingly, John prepared the way for Jesus just as the prophets did who came before him, by calling people back to the way of God. "Turn and walk toward God's horizon," John said, "for the Kingdom of God is coming!" John traveled from town to town, imploring the people of

God to listen to him, to change their hearts, to return to the ways of the covenant. As did the judges before him, John sought to persuade people to stop doing what they saw fit in their own eyes and instead live like people of the covenant. But there was something definitely new about John's message. Of all the words and phrases the judges and prophets used to communicate their message, none of them boldly claimed that the Kingdom of God was coming, that it was somehow already here. John was telling everyone to get ready, because God's Spirit was preparing to do something new.

## WHEN THE SPIRIT HITS THE STREETS

When Jesus first appeared to the disciples after the resurrection, he said, "I am sending you the gift God has promised, so stay here in the city until you receive this power." It's impossible to know what they thought this declaration meant, especially since they almost never understood what Jesus meant, but they may have considered it a pending appointment to become prophets like Isaiah or Elijah. On the day of Pentecost, some followers of Jesus, including the disciples, were gathered in Jerusalem when suddenly a rushing wind erupted and filled the room. The Holy Spirit started spreading like wildfire, resting on each of them until they began speaking in other languages, ones they didn't even know and certainly couldn't speak fluently. Because Jerusalem was a diverse city with people from many different regions and dialects living within its walls, a crowd soon began to gather in the street, bewildered because they heard their native languages being spoken by a group of likely uneducated Galileans. Nobody knew what was going on, and some people thought the miraculously fluent Galileans must be drunk. (Can you imagine—wine that immediately teaches you a foreign language? I have never seen a drunk person do anything that impressive.) In the middle of all the commotion, Peter stood up to address the crowd and said, "Hey—we're not drunk! It's only nine in the morning! This is like what the prophet Joel told us would happen! God said there would come a day when God would pour out the Spirit on everybody—on sons and daughters who would prophesy, on young and old who would see visions and dream dreams, even on servants—everybody! Everybody would become prophets!" Peter continued, telling the crowd the story of Jesus and all that had happened to him, how God had raised Jesus back to life and how they were certain that Jesus is the promised Messiah. The people listening were pierced to the heart with this news, and they asked Peter, "What should we do?" And Peter said what every person before him always said when they were filled with God's Spirit: "Turn and start walking toward God's horizon! For this promise is not just for you and your children but even for people far away from here, for God is calling all these people back home."

Within hours, the Spirit once given only to God's chosen few had filled the city of Jerusalem with three thousand prophets. God's Spirit blew open and out into the street, disregarding the boundaries of race, tribe, class, and creed. At Pentecost, the power and presence of God's Spirit exploded into the streets, making everyone who follows God prophets responsible for calling people home.

Just when we thought Easter had pretty radically expanded God's promise in a new direction, God turned around and threw a serious fireworks display at Pentecost, one that blasts God's promise so far out that the whole world can be filled with prophets. Imagine what a surprise this must have been for the disciples who had always seen the Spirit as a specially appointed power boost only given to a few people. And now, here the Spirit came blowing all over the place, making more people into prophets in one day than in all the years combined in God's story. At Pentecost, the Spirit made a quantum leap toward God's horizon.

# THE SPIRIT OF THE LIVING GOD

After a story like that, it's pretty obvious that the force of God's Spirit is not delicate. I worry that when we imagine the Holy Spirit, we picture something akin to Casper the Friendly Ghost, floating around with a smile. The very word *spirit* in our English language is misleading because the concepts we associate with the words *wind* and *spirit* are so ethereal. Our English word sounds more like the characteristically airy Romance languages than it does the throaty dialects of the Middle East. As a child I thought everything my Lebanese grandparents would say to each other in Arabic was incredibly important, because English words sounded so much more casual by comparison. The Hebrew word for spirit, *ruach*, sounds far more substantial than our *spirit*. *Ruach* is difficult for many English speakers to pronounce because you have to summon up the *ch* sound from the very back of your throat, as if you are about to spit. You have to use some guttural gravitas, some linguistic determination, as though what you are about to say is exceptionally important. It is best spoken with passionate intentionality, as if you can imagine God speaking through this *ruach* like it's a divine fiat. And actually, it is; the Spirit of God pronounces, announces, and creates the life of God. There is nothing ethereal about it.

The Spirit has always been the power of life.
The wind that swept over the chaos of the waters and
brought forth life is the same power that raised Jesus
from the dead and the same gust of wind that blew
open the doors at Pentecost and descended like flames
upon those who were gathered. It is the Spirit of the
Living God, present among us, announcing life.

Sometimes the Spirit appointed a person to
announce life in a place where things were pretty bleak.
Ezekiel had the unfortunate job of being the resident
prophet when the Temple in Jerusalem was destroyed.
Much of Israel's hopes were collected in the walls of that
Temple, and when those walls came down, their hopes
scattered. They were already displaced exiles, many of
them living in Babylon, so the destruction of the Temple
felt like the final connection to home being violently
severed. As you can imagine, most of the book of Ezekiel
is unbelievably depressing. One particularly heartbreak-
ing passage describes a dream in which Ezekiel sees God
reluctantly being led out of the Temple, slowly from
the inner Temple to the outer courts, and then from the
outer courts to the steps outside, and then to the road,
and then outside the city limits. And at every point, God
keeps looking back as if to say, "I do not want to leave.
I will not leave you. These walls may come down, but
have no fear, I will take you back. I will still claim you,
no matter what happens. I will be your God."

Later Ezekiel dreamed he was standing in the middle of a wasteland, a valley filled with dry bones. It is a chilling sight to imagine. In the dream, God asked Ezekiel, "Can these bones live?" Ezekiel looked at him, and I picture him sighing grievously as he responded, "Lord, only you know." Then God said, "Tell these bones that I will send my Spirit to fill them, and they will live." As Ezekiel spoke these words of life to the bones, a rattling sound began to reverberate as the bones began to move and come together, joint to joint, and then muscles and skin began growing, covering the bones like vines. And then God's Spirit breathed over them and on them and through them and they awakened as that Living Breath restored them to life, and they began rising to their feet in a great multitude, spanning the width of the valley. Ezekiel knew life was going to be difficult without the Temple, but in that dream God reminded him of the promise that God would always be their God and they would always be God's people. God reminded Ezekiel that even a valley of dry bones can be restored by the life-giving power of God's Spirit.

When the disciples huddled together in grief after Jesus died, they may have felt as if they too were mourning in a valley of dry bones and dried-up promises. But the risen Jesus came to them in their despair and told them to wait for a gift that would bring life not only to them, but to all the world. The Spirit of the Living God was breathing upon them, not only bringing Jesus back to life but bringing the disciples back to hope. The Spirit came to them at Pentecost and declared that their grieving bones would not only live but rise to their feet in a great multitude in the middle of Jerusalem's streets, ready to walk the way of God with renewed hope. The Spirit of God would send them out, calling them to be agents of life and hope to others.

The gift of Pentecost is the gift of the Spirit's presence with us wherever we go. It may have looked like God was being led away from us on the eve of Good Friday when Jesus headed to Golgotha, but just as God promised to Ezekiel, God has returned, this time in the unboundaried presence of the Spirit.

> The gift of Pentecost is the gift of the Spirit's presence with us wherever we go.

## TOWERS OR TURBINES?

God has invited us to be part of what the Spirit is breathing forth. As you can imagine, we don't always do this very well, which is why things like valleys of dry bones exist in the first place. Genesis 11 tells the story of when all the people of the earth gathered in one place and spoke the same language. They decided to build a city there, and a high tower reaching toward the sky, because they wanted to make a name for themselves. God looked at what they were doing and said, "This is just the beginning of what they will do; nothing they try to do will be impossible for them now." So God confused them by giving them a multitude of languages and scattered them across the earth. The city was named Babel.

Some people have made this story out to be a showdown between God and people, where God had to surprise attack us with confusing languages to keep the upper hand. To me, this is like saying the day I baby-proofed all the doors in my house was driven by some deep fear that my son Grant could now overtake me and start running the house himself. In the Babel story, God isn't scared of us—God is scared of what might happen to all of us if we go roaming out in the street with the disastrous ambition to make a name for ourselves. My friend Chris Haw once told me he can't hear the phrase, "Nothing they propose to do will be impossible for them," and not think of Hiroshima, and I think God may have felt this same way. The power of human collaboration can be both a force for great good and a force for unbearable evil. At Babel, God dethroned the people's destructive ambitions and beckoned them back toward life. God was doing us one serious favor by saving us from oppressive conformity and diversifying us instead.

At Babel, God does not only save us from ourselves, but sends us back on the path toward God's Kingdom.

That Kingdom is glimpsed on the streets of Jerusalem at the day of Pentecost, where people gathered not to build towers to make names for themselves but to be sent into the world with good news. Unlike at Babel, this time we came together in the right way and for the right purposes. At Pentecost God dismantled the boundaries and powers of race, gender, age, class, and education that stood in our way by uniting us, even in our diverse native tongues, under the common purpose of the Spirit.

Any human dictator can control a homogenous society. Only the living God can hold together a diverse global world in love.

## CONVERTING TO WIND ENERGY

If we are sent into the world as agents of the Spirit, how do we convert our individual and collective energies from building ambitious towers to creating generative wind turbines? How are we called to respond to the ways humanity has collaborated for destruction and encourage all of us to collaborate for the Kingdom instead?

In John Steinbeck's novel *The Grapes of Wrath*, there is an ongoing scene of a turtle making its way across the road. In one chapter, a man driving a truck sees the turtle and swings over to hit it, squashing its shell underneath his tires as he continues along his way. A few chapters later, Tom Joad is driving along the same road and sees a turtle in the path of his own wheels. He swerves, nearly veering the truck off the road, and the turtle safely continues his slow trek across the asphalt. Humanity's varying responses to the turtle is in many ways the central theme of Steinbeck's great work. When we find ourselves in trying times, do we become myopic in seeking our own survival? Do we become those who look out for themselves but trample others in the process? Or do we live instead as people who risk expediency and safety to ensure life? Living as people of the Spirit means that we pay more attention to the call of the Kingdom than we do to our desire to make a name for ourselves. We cannot take ourselves off the grid of human power, but if we follow the Spirit, we are called to convert that power into something that generates life for more than just our own household.

A few years ago, my husband, Dan, and I went to Hawaii. One day as we were driving along the road, I noticed a sign with an arrow saying, "Redemption Center." You probably know what this sign means, but after spending far too many hours reading theology, I saw the word *redemption* and immediately began to entertain all kinds of humorous ideas of what kind of center this might be—a drive-through confessional booth! A communion mini-mart! A passport office for heaven!

After seeing the sign a number of times over the next few days, I asked Dan to follow the arrow so that I could solve the mystery and stop the ridiculous jokes that surely were getting old. I was absolutely delighted to discover it was a recycling center. Even though I'd never heard a recycling center called a redemption center, it made perfect sense. Redemption comes from the Latin word redemptio, which literally means, "to take back." You take your aluminum cans and newspapers to the redemption center, and they take them back and make them into something new. Even though we minister types have spent semesters writing papers and reading books about God's redemption, it really isn't much more complicated than that. Redemption is the act of God taking us back and making us new. In Isaiah, God says, "Do not fear, for I have redeemed you. I have called you by name and you are mine." This is the story of God we see in Scripture: the shepherd who leaves ninety-nine sheep to go after the one who got lost in the fields, the parent who welcomes a child home with open arms after he has run away. Our God is a God who has claimed us, who is always moving further and further outward to take all of us back and make us new.

Redemption is the act of God recycling us back into who we were intended to be.

> Redemption is the act of God recycling us back into who we were intended to be.

When we take God our broken things, those parts of us we may consider expendable if not totally worthless, God doesn't keep them. Once the Spirit breathes life into them again, they come right back to us as the Spirit sends us into the world to use them for good. God gave us the Spirit at Pentecost because God wants us to be recycling centers, too. We many not have had the perfect childhood, we may have a job we hate, we may have a laundry list of vices or some intimidating character flaws. No matter. All of these things have the potential to point us toward God's horizon once the Spirit takes them back. The Spirit breathes on us so we can take the things we have been given back to God, transforming them and converting them into the kind of power that is life giving for the world. It is not only the Spirit's work to recycle the broken things of the world. God invites all of us to join in the redeeming actions the Spirit is breathing into the world. As a throng of prophets who have been unleashed in the streets to bring good news, we're called to consider how every situation, every decision, every moment given us can be recycled and become generative—that is, to become a place where new life can happen.

Just as God told the family of Abraham and Sarah that they would be blessed in order to be a blessing, the Spirit has given us gifts and abilities and called us to use them as a blessing to the world. Just like at Pentecost, our faithfulness will be found not hidden in our rooms but out on the streets, a diverse and unifying force for life that engages the world. God invites us to stand as a throng of graceful wind turbines, our arms stretching wide to respond to the movement of God's Spirit in our midst, converting our energy into gifts of life freely given to the world.

# 7

# A Whole New World

or years, the city of Austin, Texas, has circulated a
T-shirt with the slogan "Keep Austin Weird." The
shirt became so popular regionally that other Texas
cities have attempted to copy it, so that now there are
shirts reading "Keep Waco Wacky" or "Keep Lubbock
Flat." Dallas, however, was one of the first to imitate it,
probably because it was obvious what Dallas's version
would be: "Keep Dallas Pretentious." Although the shirt
is a humorous jab at the fancy houses, ritzy parties, and
haute couture that often characterize Dallas, I've always
found it to echo the religious culture of the city as well.
(And not only because churches here play "keeping up
with the Joneses" with more extravagance than most

homes could muster.) Though Dallas is not a very old city, it has a formidable religious history. Dallas's streets might not be as weathered as Philadelphia's or Boston's, but her religious towers cast a long and harrowing shadow that affects the contours of both cultural and religious life. Dallas is perhaps most famous (religiously speaking) for talking rather incessantly about what— exactly—is going to happen at the end of time, with detailed precision and unwavering conviction. I'm not sure there can be anything more pretentious than that.

We no more know what the future holds than we know what the world is like outside of our own heads. In both cases, we're stuck where we are, and that's the only vantage point we have. However, just because we don't feel pretentious enough to claim we know what the last days on earth are going to look like (or when they plan to arrive) doesn't mean we can't talk about the end of God's story. In fact, we are compelled to talk about it, because the promise hasn't moved outward all this way to begin acting now like a merry-go-round, stuck on the same annoying song as we bob along mindlessly in a circle. How in the world can we reach for a horizon in a story that isn't going anywhere?

The truth is, God's story talks frequently about the direction where all of this is heading. From the very beginning, the story of God has always been one with a future horizon. It may loop back rhythmically and thematically on itself, but its furthest edge is always moving out, pressing forward. What awaits us in these final horizon stories is not precise detail but expansive and powerful images. We don't have to turn those stories into time charts and graphs to take them seriously; in fact, I'd argue we are taking them much more to heart when we allow them to speak to us within the colorful brush strokes of imagination rather than dead-lead pencils of fatalistic destiny. And imagining God's future doesn't mean we are living in a dream world, either; it means, as my friend Doug says, that we are following after the (very real) dreams and hopes God has for the world.

There has been one central event in God's story when God gave us a sneak peek at the future, and that was the resurrection of Jesus. As New Testament scholar N.T. Wright describes, at Easter God has done for Jesus in the middle of time what God promises to do for all of us at the end of time. At the empty tomb, the boundaries of present and future fused as old creation and new creation clashed together like cymbals; old creation was pronounced finished and new creation was inaugurated at the very same time. We have already seen a true glimpse of God's future. It is not the end of the world. It is Easter.

We have already seen a true glimpse of God's future. It is not the end of the world. It is Easter.

Moving toward God's horizon means living in the tension among the boundaries of past, present, and future that have been fused together in the life of Jesus. It is to claim not only that the story has an end, but that the story's end has in some way already begun and is now pushing us out toward its full realization.

## NEW HEAVEN + NEW EARTH = NEW CREATION

The primary way Jesus followers have described the realization of God's coming future is as new creation. The prophet Isaiah declared that God will create a new heaven and a new earth where crying won't be heard in our cities, where the fields we plant will give us all the food we need, where the wolf and the lamb will eat peacefully together. Put another way, broken, unredeemed creation will be replaced by wholly redeemed creation. God declares, "Come and see! I am doing a new thing!" The old things will pass away as the new thing God is doing fully emerges. When the New Testament letters describe the new creation, earth is never abandoned as we all board the train to some faraway heaven. The new creation is when the marriage of heaven and earth becomes God's new creation, when the boundaries between the dimensions of heaven and earth will be shattered. If you think this sounds a little spacey, maybe you have always considered heaven to be too far away. Just because heaven and earth are distinct doesn't mean they are foreign to one another, or even necessarily far apart. If that sounds like we're discussing quantum theory or the possibility of multiple universes (spacey indeed!), think of it this way: I'm sure you can remember a moment when you saw a completely new dimension to someone you had known for years. You had been close to and thought you knew that person, but something changed so that you now saw the person in a different light. The impression we get and the way we are beckoned to feel about the stories of new creation are like that. It's when the God who has been near to us and known to us can be seen more fully, more clearly, more completely, and that makes everything different. The prophet Isaiah describes new creation through rich images of wolves lying peacefully among lambs and streams flowing through wastelands. Wolves and lambs and streams and deserts are all familiar to us so we can readily imagine them, but they are now placed alongside something unexpected, placed in a way that shows forth life when previously it would have brought about death.

The last book of the Bible, Revelation, invokes our imaginations as well when it describes a city where there is no need for sun or moon because the radiance of God's presence illumines everything. (Isn't that breathtaking imagery?) It proclaims the new creation by declaring, "See, God has made a home with humanity. God will dwell with them and they will be God's people." And Revelation echoes Isaiah's words when it describes Jesus declaring, "Come and see, I am making all things new!"

Revelation appeals to our imaginations, but that certainly doesn't remove it from the realities of the world. When John wrote the book of Revelation, he was living in a time when Christians were being persecuted and martyred. The emperor Domitian was the first Caesar to require all citizens to worship him as Lord. Some Christians bowed under pressure, and others, like John, revolted. The letter John wrote from prison was a call to arms, renouncing those who were cowering under pressure and prophetically calling all Jesus followers to live as God's people no matter what the cost. Of course, as a political prisoner, he couldn't call Domitian terrible names or promote imperial insurrection unless he did so very coyly, so he used symbolic language and metaphors that, though unknown to the Romans, would be readily understood by the Christian community for which it was intended. John's letter is a profound example of Christian resistance to the power of the death machines. Through rich imagery, he exposes their powers as not only evil, but more important, expired. They may be winning now, he says, but what they stand for is not eternal. John implored them to reject Emperor Domitian's horizon and follow God's instead.

Revelation is both a call to our prophetic imagination and a call to political resistance. To diminish its intent by rendering it a statement of certain prophecies that will happen at a particular appointed time in history is to greatly shrink its prophetic scope. It is a call to imagine a different kind of future, one where emperors are not allowed to kill people who refuse to worship them, one where evil systems and powers are exposed for the beasts they truly are, one where the tears of victims at the hands of their oppressors will be comforted and they will cry no more. Revelation is not a statement. It is a vision.

Revelation is not a statement. It is a vision.

I realize it's easy to become confused when reading such evocative letters as Revelation. When I was a young child, I vividly remember doing so myself. I desperately wanted to be a marine biologist and was a proud member of environmental groups such as Greenpeace, World Wildlife Fund, and the Cousteau Society. I begged my classmates and teachers to cut those plastic six-pack rings before throwing them in the trash and to buy dolphin-safe tuna. I was on a mission to save the ocean and every creature in it. I remember sitting in a pew one morning at church and, grabbing a Bible, I flipped open to Revelation and began reading. I got to the verse where it says, flatly, "And there was no more sea." There are hardly words to describe how I felt in that moment. My eyes welled up with tears, and I glared up toward the wooden ceiling beams and said very accusatorily in my head, "If you're just going to *destroy* it all, God, why in the world am I working so hard to save it? Surely I don't care about the ocean and the dolphins and the beluga whales more than *you* do, God—you *made* them!" This was my first real fight with God, my first foray into protest atheism. For days, God and I were not on speaking terms. After I cooled down, I realized I must have misunderstood the passage's intent, because God and I both knew a dolphin strangled by a plastic six-pack ring because of some lazy and indulgent human was a tragedy, or at the very least a sin, plain as day. Many years later, I read a commentary explaining that the sea was a symbol of separation and alienation. This makes perfect sense when we remember John wrote the letter while a prisoner on the island of Patmos, a place used by the Roman government to house banished political revolutionaries. The sea surrounding John's cell mocked the distance between himself and his Christian community. It symbolized the power of the Roman Empire and the consequence of rejecting Caesar as Lord. If the symbolism of sea as separation ever rang true, it did so for John those months. Far from being tragic, the metaphor of God's destruction of the sea meant good news for all creation, dolphin and human alike: God will be with us, fully, and no ruler, no empire, no government will separate us.

## LIFTING OUR VEILS

Despite its sinister connotation, the word *apocalypse* describes this very idea of God's full presence with us. *Apocalypse* literally means, "lifting the veil," so the apocalypse is the day when all that separates us from the full presence of God will be removed. Hoping for the apocalypse is like looking forward to the Great Unveiling Party. John isn't the only one to use imagery of veils in God's story. When Moses returned from speaking with God on Mount Sinai, his face was so radiant he had to wear a veil to shield the glow of God's glory from the Israelites. But whenever Moses was in God's presence, Moses removed the veil so they could speak face to face. In the New Testament letters, Paul says our hope makes us bold enough to lift our veils to everyone, and as God's radiance reflects on our faces, we become transformed into the image of God. And in his famous chapter on love, Paul says though what we now see is just a poor reflection, as in a mirror, there will come a day when we, too, will see God face to face. There will come a day when we will know God fully in the same way we are fully known by God right now. And Revelation describes the holy city, the center of new creation, prepared as a bride adorned for her beloved, and we envision our collective veils being lifted as God makes a permanent home among us. The Great Unveiling Party is the vision of the covenant promise in its fulfillment.

## A WITHERED BUSH AND A TREE OF HEALING

Just as the use of imagery evokes our hope for what is to come, prophecies evoke our desire to follow God's horizon by describing what it looks like when we don't. In God's story, prophecies are not fatalistic tarot cards letting you know if your life line is going to be long or your business successful. They are instead a study in contrasts—a way of seeing two possible endings to encourage you to stay on the right path. Prophets are the ones who look ahead and say, "If you continue doing this, it's going to start looking like that . . ." and the assumption, of course, is that nobody really wants it to look like that. Prophecies are spoken to instigate repentance, to elicit faithful response, to reorient our eyes toward God's horizon, so it's problematic if we spend all our energies analyzing the prophecy rather than experiencing it. Prophets don't roll into town with scathing words so that we will all go back to our homes and make a chart about when the ominous clouds might appear. Prophets want us to respond as if we just watched our very own personalized Greek tragedy— we should walk away seriously reconsidering what exactly we are doing with our lives, and at what price. We should wonder whether we have forgotten about the promise and realize that was not the wisest move. If we happen to forget about the promise and focus solely on the prophecy itself, making charts rather than making better future plans, we soon discover all kinds of problems. The story of Jonah shows us that.

The people of the city of Ninevah needed to be shown where their current road of indiscretion was heading, so God called a man named Jonah to go to Ninevah and call the people back to the covenant promise. Jonah didn't want to run this particular prophetic errand so at first he ran away, but after spending three days deliberating his obedience in the belly of a big fish, he conceded. When Jonah arrived in town, he gave the people of Ninevah the prophecy as God instructed. He said, "Forty days more of this business, and Ninevah's going to collapse!" When the people heard what Jonah said, the people of the city (including the king) started cleaning up their acts, wearing burlap sacks (sackcloth) to show how sorry they were and fasting for days. "Who knows?" the king told everyone. "God may change God's mind." Well, there's nothing like a good soul searching to change God's mind, so that's what happened. But it made Jonah one angry prophet. Here he had come into town, verbal guns blazing, declaring the judgment of God was imminent, and now he was going to look like a fool. Jonah told God, "I *knew* this was going to happen! This is why I didn't want to come to Ninevah in the first place! I knew you are a gracious and merciful God who doesn't get angry easily and is always eager to forgive." (Jonah was not saying this as a compliment; we quickly realize he was so completely put out by God's graciousness that he went to dramatic lengths to say so.) Jonah continued, "Just kill me, why don't you, for it's better for me to die than to live after all this." (Apparently, hell hath no fury like a prophet scorned.) God said, "Do you have any right to be this angry?" Jonah left in a huff and sulked on the outskirts of town. He waited there, hoping to see a divine fireworks show come day forty. While he waited, God made a bush grow over Jonah's head to provide him shade. Then God sent a worm to attack the bush and it withered, and then God sent a powerful east wind, and poor Jonah was now sitting in the hot sun, being blown about by the wind, angry at the fireworks show that never arrived. Jonah was beside himself. God said, "Do you have any right to be angry about the bush?" Jonah said curtly, "Yes, angry enough to *die*." Then God said, "Jonah, how is it that you can have compassion on this bush, which you didn't create and didn't grow, but you are angry that I would have compassion for Ninevah, a city of more than a hundred and twenty thousand people?"

Jonah didn't have anything to say about that.

More than the dramatic folly of his unwavering stubbornness, Jonah made one critical mistake: he valued the prophecy more than the promise. Jonah wanted the prophecy to be right more than he wanted the prophecy to be heeded. Jonah begrudged God for being gracious to Ninevah, but he sure didn't complain when God was gracious enough to grow a tree of shade over his own head. Jonah forgot that prophecies are not secret codes to be cracked or postmarked telegrams to be delivered but catalysts awakening us out of our stupors and pushing us back into movement toward God's future horizon. The best prophets are not the ones who are proven the most accurate but the ones who work themselves out of a job.

> The best prophets are not the ones who are proven the most accurate but the ones who work themselves out of a job.

When we talk about the future of God, with all of its rich and powerful prophetic images, we probably should be careful not to be stubborn like Jonah, valuing our own rightness and righteousness over God's freedom to be gracious to even the most sin-filled city. This is God's creation, and God has compassion on this world because God has labored to create it in love. If we are looking to God's future because we assume we will be safely shaded under a tree far from God's impending judgment, perhaps we have lost sight of the promise, too.

In Revelation's vision of the new creation, the river of life flows bright as crystal down the center of the city, and the tree of life stands on each side, bearing a new kind of fruit for each month of the year and providing shade to all. The leaves of the tree of life don't provide us shade so we can sit at a safe distance from the rest of new creation, thinking only of ourselves, caring only for our own righteous image. Revelation tells us the leaves of God's tree are for the healing of the nations. They are to be waved like palms as we line up along the city's wide streets, young and old, male and female, rich and poor, every tribe and tongue represented, rejoicing in the One who walks among us as Emmanuel. They are to be visible reminders of all that God has been growing among us, lush and green, as we recline in the season of God's eternal springtime, when all has blossomed forth with life.

The Kingdom of God's new creation, God's eternal springtime, embodies every hope gathered along the path of God's story. It holds the promise given to Abraham and Sarah that God will be our God and we will be God's people. It announces a future of justice and freedom to all that tries to keep us from moving forward with God. It decrees Jesus is the global King, the one who has proclaimed peace to those from east, west, north, and south. It renounces death and calls us into life. It sends us with God's Spirit as benevolent prophets, seeking to spread truly good news. And with each step, the presence of God's Spirit sends us further and further out, into the expanding world God is redeeming even now, until at last we reach that day when we will pray, "Come, Lord Jesus," and Jesus will answer us and say, "Behold, I am here."

# Epilogue

God has moved this promise a long way out from where it first began, small and unlikely, with two barren nomads getting along in age. God's promise has moved out, pulling in a random supporting cast of murderers, astrologers, grieving women, and unsuspecting people on Jerusalem's streets. If we see God's story as beginning in Genesis with creation and ending in Revelation with new creation, it's fair to say God has pointed us as far along as God intends, and now it's a matter of keeping our eyes on the horizon. God's promise comes with us, of course, as the story unfolds, and we play the part of the people who hold on to hope, who make sense of the landscape, who try to keep our eyes steady on the horizon even through the haze.

When we gather on a Sunday night at Journey, we do so for a number of reasons—we enjoy being together, we are usually eager to hear what random concoction of musical genres the band will blend together to make a hymn we've sung a million times sound brand new; we love eating dinner afterward, shoving tables together and cramming in booths and often talking quite loudly about our very strongly held positions on everything from politics to sewing techniques. But mostly, primarily, we gather to hear God's story and remember the promise. Paul once wrote that we often walk away from a mirror and forget what we look like, and we're smart enough at least to know that this is often the case. Our weeks might be filled with a million different events that cause us to question whether this promise is true, whether this God really cares, whether we are going anywhere worthwhile, and if following Jesus makes any difference. We come on Sunday to draw near God's story in an intentional way, because we don't want to walk away from our mirrors and forget whose image we're supposed to be reflecting.

In all the conversations we share as a community, we hold out hope that we might just hear of an exodus moment, an epiphany, a glimpse of resurrection, or an experience when new creation burst forth right in the middle of everything. These stories of God happen over and over, but we have to listen and pay attention to see them.

These stories of God happen over and over, but we have to listen and pay attention to see them.

122

On Sunday we come together and breathe in God's promise deeply, so that the Spirit can once again breathe us out into the world as God's people. All of life seems guided by this rhythmic breath, inhaling and exhaling, working and resting, doubting and believing, forgetting and remembering, letting things go and picking things up. In whatever way we understand worship, I think at its most fundamental level it is the act of holy breathing. We know how much in this world, in ourselves, attempts to constrict our airways and separate us from the One who breathes life into our lungs. The holy inhalation of gathering under God's promise is the way we take God's story back from all that tries to shrink it; it's the way we open up space in ourselves, in our communities, in our world, so that the wind of God's Spirit can freely disperse us forward. It's the way we make sure the story of God's promise stays as big as the promise itself.

I saw a church video once that distinguished the difference between the metaphor of the church as a cruise ship (Is it fun here? Do they have a variety of activities?) and a battleship (Is their purpose clear? Is the captain trustworthy?). Though the video made the case for the battleship metaphor, I prefer to think of the church, God's gathered and gathering people, as something more akin to a sailboat. Rather than a behemoth mass of steel with karaoke machines or (worse) weapons aboard, sailboats rely primarily on the wind to propel them forward. Despite the unruly waves of the sea, we try to trust that the wind of God's Spirit will get us where we need to go.

I mentioned this thought to a friend of mine who sighed as she said, "That's probably true, but it sure feels rickety sometimes out on this boat," and I have to agree with her. It probably explains why we often do so many things to try to make this journey toward God's horizon feel more secure, but I wonder if that doesn't keep us from having to do the very important work of remembering the promise, even if we're a little breathless sometimes out here on the waves. We may start believing that we need buildings or doctrines or hierarchies or prophetic time charts to keep this story going. We may start building these things in the hopes of following God only to realize we've really ended up making names for ourselves.

I'm quite certain even the little communal sailboat that I pastor is probably doing this even now, but I hope we are honest enough with each other to say so and to put down our ambitious hammers and once again sit back down and tend to the sails. I hope we learn to live as people who truly believe the promise is big enough, that the promise is sending us further out into God's story this very moment. I hope in times of troubled waters we remember that Jesus asked his followers to step out of their small boat and have faith to walk on the water, and I hope, if push comes to shove, we'd abandon even our beloved little sailboat to walk toward God's outstretched hand, too.

In all the ways we have understood what it means to be God's people through the years, I pray we can remember that we have always been people of hope. We have always been the people who have dared to believe in God's promises, even and perhaps most important when they seem rather far-fetched. I hope the winds of cynicism never outmatch the billowing promise that has filled our sails as long as this story's been told, because only the promise leads us to that place where all of us find our rightful home with our God.

We have always been the people who have dared to believe in God's promises.

# Notes

### Chapter One: The Universe Is Moving Outward

If you are interested in learning more about the universe, I recommend *The Elegant Universe* by Brian Greene (New York: Norton, 1999). It is accessible even to those of us who are unfamiliar with scientific terminology.

You can read the story of Abraham and Sarah beginning in Genesis 12.

### Chapter Two: The God of Green Lights

You can read the entire story of the Israelites' journey from slavery to the Promised Land in the Book of Exodus, the second book in the Bible.

Ann Belford Ulanov and Barry Ulanov, *The Healing Imagination* (New York: Daimon Verlag Press, 1991).

Moses' speech is in Deuteronomy 30:11–20.

For more information regarding microfinance, I suggest reading Muhammad Yunus, *Banker to the Poor* (New York: Public Affairs Press, 2003). You may also be interested in visiting the Web site, www.kiva.org, where you can support microfinance efforts around the world.

Visit www.invisiblechildren.com to read more about the plight of child soldiers in Uganda and to support their efforts.

### Chapter Three: We Come Bearing Gifts

The story of the astrologers can be found in Luke 2:25.

The parable of the banquet is in Luke 14.

Paul's words about Jesus bringing peace to those far and near is from Ephesians 2.

### Chapter Four: From Gatekeepers to Door Openers

Melchizedek appears in Genesis 14:18–19, and you can also find references to him in Hebrews 5–11.

The story of Jethro and Moses is in Exodus 19.

The story of the Temple curtain tearing in two can be found in Matthew 27, Mark 15, and Luke 23.

Thanks to Pete Rollins for his thoughts on Jesus' genealogy. See Peter Rollins, *The Fidelity of Betrayal* (Brewster, Mass.: Paraclete Press, 2008).

Jesus' declaration of being the gate is from John 10.

### Chapter Five: When the End Is Just the Beginning

The story of the woman anointing Jesus with oil is in John 12.

Luke 10 tells the parable of the Good Samaritan.

The story of the Maccabean revolt is in the apocryphal book of 1 Maccabees.

For a fantastic resource on a Christian response to poverty see Ronald J. Sider, *Rich Christians in an Age of Hunger* (Nashville, Tenn.: Word, 1997).

## Chapter Six: Wind Power

The story of Pentecost is in Acts 2.

Ezekiel 37 tells the vision of the valley of dry bones.

Thanks to Chris Haw for his insightful comment about Babel during a conversation we had in Florida in 2008. Chris Haw and Shane Claiborne addressed the story of Babel in their book, *Jesus for President* (Grand Rapids, Mich.: Zondervan, 2008). See pp. 30–31 for his comments on Babel.

John Steinbeck, *The Grapes of Wrath* (New York: Penguin, 1939).

## Chapter Seven: A Whole New World

N. T. Wright, *Surprised by Hope* (San Francisco: HarperOne, 2008), p. 93. I could not be more thankful for this book, which addresses and seeks to correct the major misunderstandings of heaven, resurrection, and the coming of God in a wonderfully concise way.

Visions of the new creation mentioned in this chapter can be read in Isaiah 65 and 43 and Revelation 21 and 22.

Passages with veil imagery are in Exodus 34:29–32, 2 Corinthians 3:12ff, and 1 Corinthians 13:12–13.

Jonah's story is a small book by the same name in the Old Testament.

# The Author

Danielle Shroyer is pastor of Journey Community Church in Dallas, Texas, a holistic missional Christian community (www.journeydallas.com). She has been involved in Emergent Village for over a decade and also helps facilitate the Dallas Emergent Cohort (www.emergentdallas.blogspot.com). Shroyer is an honors graduate of Baylor University, where she earned her bachelor of arts degree with a double major in religion and speech communication. She then attended Princeton Theological Seminary, where she earned her master of divinity degree. An ordained minister, Shroyer has served in numerous roles, including university chaplain, youth minister, contemporary church staff minister, and assistant chaplain of a retirement community. She and her husband, Dan, have two children, Mia and Grant.

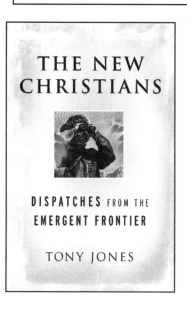

# THE NEW CHRISTIANS

Dispatches from the Emergent Frontier

## Tony Jones

ISBN 978-0-470-45539-5
Paperback | 288 pp

*"Jones provides the single best introduction to the Emergent Church movement."*
—Publishers Weekly

Through stories and "dispatches" about the many adventurous communities and practices of emergent Christians around the world, Tony Jones offers an in-depth view of this new "third way" of faith between religious conservatism and religious liberalism.

With the depth of theological expertise and broad perspective he has gained as a pastor, writer, theologian, and leader of the movement, Jones initiates readers into the emergent conversation and offers a new way forward for all Christians. Written with a journalist's flair and a participant's studied reflection, this fascinating book draws upon years of research to provide compelling examples and first-hand stories of who is doing what, where, and why it matters.

**TONY JONES (tonyj.net)** is the author of many books on Christian ministry and spirituality, including *The Sacred Way: Spiritual Practices for Everyday Life.* He is a theologian-in-residence at Solomon's Porch in Minneapolis and a doctoral fellow in practical theology at Princeton Theological Seminary. Tony is a sought-after speaker and consultant in the areas of emerging church, postmodernism, and Christian spirituality.

## A CHRISTIANITY WORTH BELIEVING

Hope-Filled, Open-Armed, Alive-and-Well Faith

### Doug Pagitt

ISBN 978-0-470-45534-0
Paperback | 256 pp

"A Christianity Worth Believing *is a guide for Christians who doubt their own faith but are not yet ready to give up on it all. Seeking to inspire souls to find their faith once more by addressing common problems and answering the questions not normally answered, [it] is a choice pick for anyone who wants to reclaim their religion.*" —Midwest Book Review

*A Christianity Worth Believing* offers an engaging, 'come-with-me-on-a-journey-of-exploring-the-possibilities' approach to what it means to be a follower of Jesus in our day. Written by Doug Pagitt—a leading voice in the Emergent conversation—this beautifully written book weaves together theological reflections, Christian history, and his own story of faith transformation.

**DOUG PAGITT** is the pastor of Solomon's Porch, a holistic, missional Christian community in Minneapolis, Minnesota. He has written a number of books, has worked in churches and for a non-profit foundation, and owns two businesses in Minneapolis. Doug is a sought-after speaker for churches, denominations, and businesses throughout the United States and around the world on issues of culture and Christianity. He can be reached at **www.DougPagitt.com**.

## SOUL GRAFFITI

Making a Life in the Way of Jesus

Mark Scandrette

ISBN 978-0-470-27662-4
Paperback | 272 pp

*"Mark Scandrette guides us in this beautifully written and brilliantly illustrated book along a path towards actualized spirituality in a postmodern world. The book provides new avenues to ancient truths."*
—Tony Campolo, professor of sociology, Eastern University

*Soul Graffiti's* simple and lyrical exploration of the essential message of Jesus as it relates to the experiences of contemporary spiritual seekers integrates theological insight with awareness of human psychology, culture, and daily life. Written to appeal to the sensibilities of those who inhabit a post-Christendom milieu, Mark Scandrette's deepest hope is to give readers greater motivation for, and a fuller sense of what it means to make a life in, the way of Jesus.

**MARK SCANDRETTE** is the executive director and cofounder of ReIMAGINE, a center for spiritual formation in San Francisco. Mark is a founding member of SEVEN, a monastic community devoted to holistic and integrative Christian spirituality. With extensive experience leading churches and community-based organizations, Mark has been a minister, writer, and spiritual teacher for 15 years. Mark is also a senior fellow with Emergent (www.emergentvillage.com), a growing generative friendship among missional Christian leaders.

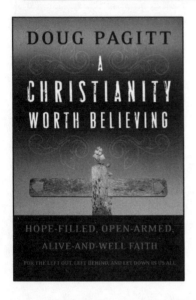

## A CHRISTIANITY WORTH BELIEVING

Hope-Filled, Open-Armed, Alive-and-Well Faith

Doug Pagitt

ISBN 978-0-470-45534-0
Paperback | 256 pp

"A Christianity Worth Believing *is a guide for Christians who doubt their own faith but are not yet ready to give up on it all. Seeking to inspire souls to find their faith once more by addressing common problems and answering the questions not normally answered, [it] is a choice pick for anyone who wants to reclaim their religion."* —Midwest Book Review

*A Christianity Worth Believing* offers an engaging, 'come-with-me-on-a-journey-of-exploring-the-possibilities' approach to what it means to be a follower of Jesus in our day. Written by Doug Pagitt—a leading voice in the Emergent conversation—this beautifully written book weaves together theological reflections, Christian history, and his own story of faith transformation.

**DOUG PAGITT** is the pastor of Solomon's Porch, a holistic, missional Christian community in Minneapolis, Minnesota. He has written a number of books, has worked in churches and for a non-profit foundation, and owns two businesses in Minneapolis. Doug is a sought-after speaker for churches, denominations, and businesses throughout the United States and around the world on issues of culture and Christianity. He can be reached at **www.DougPagitt.com**.